POCKET EDITION

Published from
Mardukite Borsippa HQ, San Luis Valley, Colorado
Founding Church of Mardukite Zuism,
Mardukite Academy & Systemology Society
for religious and educational purposes only.

MERLYN STONE'S LOST CLASSIC RESTORED

THE WITCH'S HANDBOOK

A COMPLETE GRIMOIRE OF WITCHCRAFT

by Joshua Free writing as Merlyn Stone
Edited and Introduced by Rowen Gardner

THE JOSHUA FREE IMPRINT
JFI PUBLICATIONS

© 2022, JOSHUA FREE

ISBN : 979-8-9864379-5-8

A special pocket version of
The Witch's Handbook
dedicated to Fairuza Balk

Pocket Paperback Edition — *July 2022*

Also available in hardcover

mardukite.com

A <u>Classic</u> of 20th Century Witchcraft

Once intended as a sequel to "The Sorcerer's Handbook" by Joshua Free while writing as "Merlyn Stone" in the 1990's, his "notebooks" composing the historically legendary "1998 Book of Shadows" – and now "The Witch's Handbook" – were only released privately to members of his own coven in Colorado.

Among the many facets explored within these pages, you will also encounter the complete structure of the original century-old "Book of Shadows," illuminated for the first time with a new revolutionary *never-before-published* presentation of concise descriptions and references that uncover influential behind-the-scenes sources of many contemporary Wiccan and traditionalist Witchcraft movements.

Rites of Initiation, Elemental Consecrations, Sacred Tools, Herbs, Sabbat Ceremonies, Ritual Magic, Spellcraft... It's all here!

From the *Key to Solomon*, to the *Rites of the Golden Dawn* and OTO, to the *Aradian Gospel of Witches*, to the relatively modern innovation of a "Neopagan Eightfold Year" by three men: a Druid (*Ross Nichols*), a Magician (*Aleister Crowley*) & a Witch (*Gerald Gardner*); an underlying story unfolds beneath and back of the 20th Century Witchcraft revival and no stone or pentacle is left unturned in this effective, yet candid, complete practical guide to the true "Arts of Witchcraft."

Long-standing and returning fans will celebrate the release of "The Witch's Handbook" as the missing link of a once proposed "Merlyn Stone" trilogy from the 1990's, which includes "The Sorcerer's Handbook" and "The Druid's Handbook" – both of which have already been widely accepted in the underground "New Age" scene.

This special pocket paperback reissue is dedicated by the author to *Fairuza Balk* and, as a bonus, features Joshua Free's tribute to "The Craft" movie, including his previously unpublished treatment of its practical witchcraft as "Nancy's Book of Shadows."

TABLET OF CONTENTS

SABBATS AND GROVE FESTIVALS

THE ARTS OF SPELLCRAFT

RITES OF INITIATION

APPENDIX

A TREASURY OF TRADITIONAL
20TH CENTURY WITCHCRAFT

introduction by Rowen Gardner

Once intended a sequel to *"The Sorcerer's Handbook"* by Joshua Free while writing as "Merlyn Stone" in the 1990's, his "notebooks" composing the historically legendary *"1998 Book of Shadows"*—and eventually *"The Witch's Handbook"*— were only released privately to members of his own *Coven* operating in Colorado, and other groups he networked with, during a peak period of development for the modern "New Age."

Within these pages, you will also encounter the complete structure of the original century-old *"Book of Shadows,"* illuminated for the first time with a new revolutionary *never before published* presentation of concise descriptions and references that uncover influential sources behind-the-scenes of many contemporary *Wiccan* and traditionalist *Witchcraft* movements. It's all here.

From the *Key of Solomon*, to the *Rites of the Golden Dawn* and *OTO*, to the *Aradian Gospel of Witches*, to the relatively modern innovation of a "Neopagan Eightfold Year" by three men: a Druid (Ross Nichols), a Magician (Aleister Crowley) and a Witch (Gerald Gardner); no stone or pentacle is left unturned in this effective, yet candid, complete practical guide to the *Arts of Witchcraft*.

Long before the public inception of the *Systemology Society*, or even the *Mardukite Research Organization*, Joshua Free maintained an underground occult presence in the 1990's as "Merlyn Stone." Thousands of copies of his works began circulating during an era prior to the type of commercialized self-publishing and "print-on-demand" distribution prevalent throughout the "New Age" market today. At the time, it was still quite a prestigious feat to see hundreds of handmade books reaching new readers each month— but what's more amazing is that Joshua Free (then "Merlyn Stone") was *only* a high school teenager.

Although it is quite common for writers to maintain an archival stock of unpublished notebooks and manuscripts, "*The Witch's Handbook*" is unique for the fact that its existence as the "*1998 Book of Shadows*" is not altogether unknown. But since it was rarely referred to and never officially circulated outside the personal contact of its author, we can now finally treat this complete version of the work as a "lost classic restored" more than two decades since its first underground presentation. It is also unique fro the fact that it is the *only* book ever written by Joshua Free dedicated exclusively to *Wicca* and *Witchcraft*.

Some readers and long-time Seekers following along with Joshua Free's metaphysical literary releases over the past twenty years may recall sparse allusions to the "*1998 Book of Shadows*" or a secret unpublished "*Sorcerer's Notebook*" appearing throughout his works, including the recent reissue of "*Elvenomicon*" (formerly "*Book of Elven-Faerie*") and "*The Great Magickal Arcanum: A Master Course in Magick for Modern Wizards.*" But very little is known about the original work, in spite of excerpts appearing in an Appendix for the latest 21st Anniversary Collector's Edition of "*The Sorcerer's Handbook,*" with a footnote that simply reads:

> "Commissioned in 1998 by the 'Outer Court' (or training coven) of the *Elven Fellowship Circle of Magick* (*EFCOM*) in Denver, which was integrated into their Book of Shadows."

Much like Joshua Free's *Draconomicon*—which I was also called on to produce a Foreword for when it was recently reissued in an expanded and enhanced 25th Anniversary Collector's Edition—originally "*The Witch's Handbook*" was not written or even intended for mass circulation when it first appeared underground as penned by "Merlyn Stone," a name the author primarily operated with in the "New Age" from 1995 until 2005, prior to the launch of "Mardukite Ministries" (Mardukite

Zuism) or founding the "Systemology Society."

It is due to the circulation of *Draconomicon* in the 1990's during the "Merlyn Stone Era" that I was able to be acquainted with the prodigious work of Joshua Free, much of which is only now being given its due attention and credit by the more mainstream contemporary "New Age" community. And there are a few others that were privileged to experience similar encounters with the author during his early period of development in the 1990's —yet many of us surprisingly and cautiously alarmed when coming around to face a *teenager* not even out of high school. However, these many decades later, I have resolved that my faith was well-placed in the young *lad*.

Yet, "faith" is something that has never been requested by Joshua Free in all of his deliveries and apprenticeships. Where it comes to "magick" and "metaphysics," he always provides a certain flavor of candid blatant pragmatism that is generally not seen in most presentations of the occult—and of which it is apparent over the past decade that many have borrowed heavily from his examples of establishing an "internet presence" long before such was commonplace. As a result, he stands apart from the growing numbers of pseudo-gurus and flashy web-based occult niches that really have provided little of true value to anyone—and the subject of "Witchcraft" is no exception.

A strange sensation comes over me, given my background, when given this opportunity to assist in editing the first ever public release of "*The Witch's Handbook*" for what is assumed to be a predominantly North American readership. For one thing: I am writing from Wales, or what many across the pond refer to simply as part of "England" or "Britain"—and it is not very far from where I sit that Gerald Gardner (of no known family relation to me, by the way, though I've never looked into it very closely) was first "initiated" into what was, at the time, "*English Witchcraft*," and of which has become quite popular in America as "*Wicca.*"

It is, however, curious to me that now—twenty years into the new millennium—so little of our traditional *Witchcraft* from England remains in the poorly copied watered-down rehashes pushed in the "New Age" market today, and which when compared to the literature available and traditions active during the 1900's, offer far less genuine substance for a Seeker, or in this case: *Aspiring Witch*. It is for this very reason that when the pages resurfaced again in discussion—as Joshua Free was preparing to deliver 48 lectures for the "*Mardukite Master Course*" in September 2020—I pressed the idea for the work to finally be published and even volunteered to edit and arrange the contents.

The reluctance to publish this book, according to my discussion with Joshua Free, has never been concerning the validity or merit of the work itself. However, shortly after initial commercial novelty of "*The Sorcerer's Handbook*" began to wane in 2001, Joshua Free's continuing underground pursuits—up to the point of launching the "Mardukite" movement—were dedicated exclusively to Druidism and tracking its evolution back to Mesopotamia.

Even after his return to the public scene in 2008, with the exception of *Sorcerer's Handbook* and *Great Magickal Arcanum*, all of his published books indeed surrounded the Druids and/or Babylon—leaving out his little know work on *Witchcraft* as an anomaly. As he said to me, "quite frankly, it's been two decades since I've had any interaction with the *Wiccan* community directly and I'm not sure that they would even take serious notice of this work." Yet, after seeing what passes for "*authentic Witchcraft*" these days, I beg to differ.

This premiere edition of *The Witch's Handbook* is based on the original notebooks, offering far greater detail than the literal hand-written hardcover "*1998 Book of Shadows*" that was copied and circulated nearly a quarter-of-a-century ago. It is already established in other works that the "*1998 Book of Shadows*" was intended primarily for

"Outer Court" or "training" purposes of the *Elven Fellowship Circle of Magick* and other networking groups; but Joshua Free also prepared and released each of the main sections—as it appears in *The Witch's Handbook*—separate from one another as incremental installments throughout 1998 for inclusion in the greater body of the "EFCOM" *Book of Shadows*.

Those readers familiar with the literary works by Joshua Free will more readily recognize some of the elements found within this background for *The Witch's Handbook*, which otherwise may be misinterpreted as "just one more *Wicca* book on the shelves." This one is different; and it already has its own place within a long prestigious legacy of occult instruction by one of the most profound voices on the planet today—and it is that unique quality of voice that is able to bring a new illumination to a subject that has been all but beaten to death by just about every writer that has had a stab at it.

The Witch's Handbook is also an unknown (yet integral) part of early developmental work that others are likely to recognize, including: *The Sorcerer's Handbook* and *Great Magickal Arcanum*. Although distinctions have blurred in recent reissues: facets of the first edition *Sorcerer's Handbook* (Spring 1998) and the second edition (as "*The Witch's Handbook*" or "*1998 Book of Shad-*

18

ows") were combined for the *Sorcerer's Notebook*, released publicly as the third edition *Sorcerer's Handbook* (Autumn 1998), which received the greatest circulation of all versions of the *Sorcerer'-s* Handbook, with nearly two-thousand copies in print by 2001. But aside from the title, none of these early editions actually resembled one another —and only two have ever been released publicly before now.

The Witch's Handbook is the "missing link" of a once proposed "Merlyn Stone" trilogy that includes *The Sorcerer's Handbook* and *The Druid's Handbook*—both of which have been widely accepted in the underground "New Age" scene already. When one considers that yet another remnant of Joshua Free's unpublished 1990's occultism reemerged, revised and expanded, five years ago under a pretense of *The Vampyre's Handbook*, it has become increasingly clear to me that it is high time that *The Witch's Handbook* also receive inclusion among the rapidly expanding catalog of his works.

Within the pages of *The Witch's Handbook*, an underlying story unfolds beneath and back of the 20th Century revival of *Witchcraft*—and yet the elements of its nature may not become obvious to the reader until the first complete pass through its entirety. True, there are many "Elders of the Craft" still alive that may find no new surprises or "secrets" embedded within this tome; yet even these folk will assuredly enjoy refreshing amusement in the candid *authenticity* present in its relay —something all but lost today in the endless pop-art rehashes of *Wicca* or *Witchcraft* "new releases" now marketed to curious Seekers.

The Witch's Handbook presents a "Traditionalist" approach to *Wicca* and *Witchcraft*—once more prominently visible in America during revivals of the 1900's as "*Gardnerian*" and "*Alexandrian*" traditions were imported. Of course, once they reached the states, the scene changed from "*Traditionalist Wicca*" to "*American Witchcraft*"— particularly as the "New Age" movements progressively expanded during the 1960's through the 1970's. By the 1980's, traditions of "*American Witchcraft*" hardly resembled flavors of the original "*Wiccan*" contributions—as sparse as they may be—from those like Gerald Gardner, Aleister Crowley, Ross Nichols and Doreen Valiente through the 1950's and early 1960's, once the "Anti-Witchcraft Laws" were repealed in England in 1951.

In Ireland and Britain, the phrase "Old Religion" refers to remnants from Celtic culture and customs indigenous to our lands—and its people—long before the rise of traditional Christianity. In many respects, this work is considered "Druidic" or *of the Druids*; a class of superior learned individuals responsible for maintaining functional "systems" of ancient "*Keltia*"—the Celtic territories they governed, which at one point extended from our familiar Western Isles all the way to "Anatolia" (or present-day Turkey). There are many ways in which the "Old Religion" reflects what is found in other ancient societies—such as with the Ancient Near East—and their practice of using mystical religion as a backbone to civic systematization.*

But *times do change* and a tradition must be able to synchronously evolve for it to remain relevant to its practitioners and their environment... and also *survive*.

During the 20th Century, considerable P.R. ("public relations") efforts and other "New Age" publicity assistance ushered in a new era where the idea of "*Wicca*" and "*Witchcraft*" would be looked upon more favorably in the mainstream. Of course, many of the same dogmatic stigmas still apply when treating "paganism" in contrast to two millennium of orthodox opposition. But, even in

---

* For additional details and background regarding information in this paragraph, refer to the "*Druidic*" material by Joshua Free, including "*Draconomicon*"—which is also reprinted in the Master Edition anthology: "*Merlyn's Complete Book of Druidism.*

most distant times—at the inception of language and civilized systems in Mesopotamia—the idea of "*Witches*" and "*Sorcerers*" were treated negatively even from within this archetypal "magical" society.‡

Ancient "magical societies" were often "temple-centric." The governing "religious" institutions worked closely with ruling powers and the general populace in establishing a cohesive civic and cultural system. Here we see "esoteric knowledge" preserved within the ranks of "*Priestcraft*"— which includes quite elaborate traditions of *Priestesses* serving in dedication of a *Starry Goddess*. But all of this was strictly maintained by "*Initiates*" of the Temple within an urban environment and infrastructure. The seepage of this lore into the hands of "outsiders" and "exiles" took place *afterward*, the likes of which were treated as anathema by the "State."

Unlike what we might encounter with the last 2,000 years of history—where practice of all "magic" is "evil"—the "negative connotations" first attached to "*Witches*" and "*Sorcerers*" in ancient Mesopotamia related to a much deeper standard

‡ As expressed by Joshua Free in his introductory statements to "*The Maqlu Ritual Book*" —which is also reprinted in "*Practical Babylonian Magic*" and the Master Edition anthology "*Necronomicon: The Complete Anunnaki Legacy.*"

regarding "unsanctioned magic" practiced *outside* the Temple for personal gain *separate* from the societal system.

Therefore, even at its semantic inception, practice of "*witchcraft*" is a demonstration of *personal* spiritual and magical "religious" tradition that detours the governing infrastructure of its cultural knowledge source. We can even assume that many such individuals were also once proper *Initiates* themselves—"sanctioned" *Priests* and *Priestesses* of these famous ancient civilizations—but later left these Temple ranks (and perhaps urban life altogether), taking their knowledge with them into the rural countryside and wilderness.

Of course, were it not for these rebellious efforts throughout the past several millennium, we would perhaps find far fewer genuine traces and active practices of the ancient legacy surviving into present time. While the political structure of civilizations has risen and fallen—and new gods replaced the old—remnants of the "Old Religion" and its folklore continued onward only in far distant reaches of the human population; among those who were not satisfied to accept sweeping societal changes taking place at the whims of a few war generals and tyrant emperors. Because, since when did the masses ever know best for the greater whole—and since when did "might become right"?

The Wheel turns...

◇ ◇ ◇ ◇ ◇ ◇ ◇

To our benefit today, it is both curious and practical that Joshua Free would archive so many citations of source material in his notebooks of "*Traditional European Wicca,*" when the practical demonstrations and advisement to *Covens* and *Groves* found throughout his better known works on "Western Magical Tradition" would suggest a personal background and propagation of "*American Witchcraft,*" of which he was certainly immersed in during the mid-1990's. This is why the esoteric scholarship collected within our newly restored version of *The Witch's Handbook* is worthy of attention, perhaps even more so now in the 21st Century. It will undoubtedly also be of special interest to those Seekers that have been closely examining the timeline of developments for his unique brand and "*gradient path,*" which is now instructed formally from the *Mardukite Academy.*

The Witch's Handbook is a key component of the "Merlynomian Tradition" established by Joshua Free, while writing as Merlyn Stone, in the 1990's; and it is notable supplemental to the "Grade-I Route-A" presentation of "Magick & Mysticism" that is otherwise available as *The Great Magickal Arcanum: A Master Course in Magick for Modern*

24

Wizards. As a critical volume of the "Merlyn's Magick" collection—intended for release alongside *Sorcerer's Handbook*, *Druid's Handbook* and even *Draconomicon*—this new presentation of *The Witch's Handbook* is sure to become a treasured component of your personal esoteric library.

Wishing you the best, from the arms of the Dragon.

—Rowen Gardner
Winter Solstice 2020
Wales, U.K.

ROLE & POWER OF WITCHES
(Aradian Tradition)

And then it came to pass that Diana, once her daughter Aradia had accomplished her mission (or completed her allotted time) on the Earth planet among the Humans, recalled her back to the Other. And Aradia was given powers to bestow upon those deserving mortals—and that a Witch conjuring her, one that has performed good deeds and invokes her name, may be granted the power:

—To be successful in love.[∞]
—To do good or evil.[‡]
—To converse with spirits.
—To find hidden treasure (in ancient ruins).
—To understand the voice of the wind.
—To change water into wine.
—To divine with cards.
—To know the secrets of the hand.[*]
—To cure diseases.
—To beautify those who are ugly.
—To tame wild beasts.

[∞] (And grant others to be successful in love.)
[‡] "To bless friends with power or curse enemies."
[*] "Palm reading" (*palmistry*).

And if ye be in the favor of Aradia, whatsoever ye ask shall be granted. The Witch invokes Aradia in dedication and devotion when calling out... *I Seek Aradia, Aradia, Aradia!*

—THE BOOK OF ARADIA

THE WITCH'S
HANDBOOK

RITES OF CONSECRATION
(Merlyn Stone, Autumn '98)

Here we discus "consecrations." To *consecrate* is "*to make sacred*"—an ability entirely within the personal domain; spiritual (or mental, if you prefer) creative faculties of the *Witch*. It is within the power of the *Priestess* or *Priest* to *sanctify*, to "*make clean and holy*" and to treat the instruments and things necessary to be used in the *Art of Witchcraft*.

> "*The virtue of this Consecration primarily consists of two things; to wit, in the power of the person consecrating, and by virtue of the prayer by which the Consecration is made. For in the person consecrating, there is required holiness of Life, and power of sanctifying—which are acquired by priestly offices and initiation. And that the person should, with a firm and undoubted faith, believe the virtue, power and efficacy hereof.*

> "*There is also use of the invocation of some Divine names, with the consignation of holy Seals, and things of the sort, which are conducive to sanctification and expiation; such as are the sprinkling with Holy-Water, unctions with Holy-Oil, and odorife-*

> *rous burning of incense—all appertaining to holy Worship—used everywhere with holy Wax-lights or Lamps burning; for without Lights, no sacrament is rightly performed.*"[1]

All significances of "things" are attributed from *Self*—and it is only by definitive—or Self-determined—*attentions* (directed *intentionally* as "actual" *Awareness*) that a "thing" *is realized* as "*sacred*"; and by this term "sacred" we mean: that which is acknowledged to represent or reflect the "Divine"—or else, "higher" *spiritual* truths behind all *apparent* existence. This is subject only to the very *considerations* held by *Self*, a spiritual (primary) *action* projected as *thought* (and subsequently demonstrated as material *action*). Observance of "Causal Law" or "Natural Law" is paramount to the *Craft*.

OF THE WATER & SALT

The Elements (and conditions) of *Water* and *Salt* (*Earth*) are indicative of physical solidity and substance—or "*form*"—manifest in *apparent* existence on the *Earth Planet* (represented as the "Mother" in most traditions). *Water* and *Earth* are

---

1   Quoting from Henry Cornelius Agrippa, *Of Magical Ceremonies: The Fourth Book of Occult Philosophy.*

also the most "feminine" aspects of the Divine when we derive core "magickal correspondences" from "elemental" knowledge (concerning Nature and natural philosophy). Traditionally, this *Water* and *Salt* (once consecrated) become ingredients for baking a simple bread or cake during the ritual, to be shared in "communion" among those present in the *Coven* or *Grove* gathering.

A *Bowl of Water* and *Bowl of Salt* are set on the *Altar*—or, the *Salt* (or *Sea-Salt*) may be cupped in a *Seashell*. During the consecration, each *Bowl* may be respectively placed on the *Pentacle* or a "consecration stone" (used as a *focal*; an assist to concentrate mental focus).

Original suggestions from the "*Book of Aradia*" promoted the *Athame* (or ritual *Dagger*) as the traditional "active" elemental ritual tool for *witchcraft*, although many practitioners exclusively use a *Wand* during ceremonial applications. As practical needs for personal (physical) "protection" increased amongst practitioners, it is quite possible that *Witches* began carrying a *Dagger/Athame* to substitute *Wands* as their key implement of the "air element."

Many ritual suggestions that appear in *The Witch's Handbook* are derived from the *Gardnerian Book of Shadows* from the early 20th century—which was itself based heavily on the "*Book of Aradia*" and "*Key of Solomon*" (and other "*grimoires*" from the Middle Ages), but with a removal of many complicated formulas, including use of *Kabbalah* and other lengthy roll-calls of *Hebrew-Semitic* "Names" for spirits or the Divine.

As opposed to a strict "folk charm" variety of spells and potions that is often conjured to mind in regards to the *Craft*, traditional modern *Wicca-Witchcraft* (since the early 1900's) often incorporates and simplifies "ceremonial magic" note-books (equally set within a Judeo-Christian world-view), which are then overlaid with a particular "religious mythographic semantic set"—such as with *Gardnerian* traditions, which include *Aradia* and *Kernunnos* (or *Cernunnos*) as primary repres-entatives of the "Divine" ("Goddess" and "God").[‡] In older "*grimoires*," as many as 72 names of spir-its (or deities) might be intoned for any one "con-juration" or "incantation." In many modern tradi-tions, long lists of deities from various cultural mythologies are often substituted.

The *Witch* (or *High Priestess*) dips the point-tip of the *Athame* into the *Bowl of Water*, saying:

[‡] Particularly a *lunar* or *crescent-horned* "*goddess*" and a *horned* or *antlered-headed* "*god*," of which *Kernunnos* also represents in Celtic/Druidic traditions as "Forest God of the Wilds" shown with *antlers* for *horns*.

"I conjure[∞] thee, O Creature of Water, that thou cast out from thee all the impurities and uncleanness of the spirits of the world of phantasm; in the names of … and …"[2]

The *Witch* (or *High Priest*) then dips the point-tip of the *Athame* into the *Bowl of Salt*, saying:[∫]

"Blessings be upon this Creature of Salt; let all malignity and hindrance be cast forth thencefrom, and let all good enter therein. Wherefore I bless thee and invoke thee, that you may aid me; in the names of … and …"[3]

∞   The original word here, from the *Key of Solomon*, is "*exorcise.*"

2   "May all which is evil, all which is negative, all which is base and harmful, be cast forth from this creature of earth, never to return. May only that which is, that which is clean and noble, remain within."—Ed Fitch, *Grimoire of Shadows*.
   "Element of water, I do banish and cast from thee all that is impure and unclean, that thou may be a fitting tool for our magickal use; and I do charge thee in the names of the God and Goddess."—Mary Kay Simms, *The Witch's Circle*.

∫   Some traditions simply apply a variation of the incantation for *Water* to the *Salt/Earth*, and then tools representing *Air* and *Fire*, &tc.

3   "Take a goblet of water, holding it up to the west and say, 'May the Spirits of Water bestow their blessing and remember.' Take the bowl of salt and

In some traditions, a pinch of consecrated *Salt* is sprinkled at the four corners of the *Altar.* Incorporation of the *Water* and *Salt* in the *Chalice* is treated as part of the "Great Rite."

OF THE GREAT RITE

Traditionally, the "Great Rite" signifies "sexual magic" and "alchemical union"—the creative generative force represented by the "*hiero gamos*" or "sacred marriage" of the *Divine* (*God* and *Goddess*) in this universe. Many archaic sources also allude to physical acts (between the *High Priest* and *High Priestess*) subsequent to symbolic rites utilizing the *Chalice* and *Athame* (*Dagger*). Of course, observation of the original practice among clergy now varies widely between traditions. Additional aspects of the "Great Rite" practice are also applied to the "Third Degree Initiation" (in *Gardnerian* tradition).

The "Great Rite" is integral to a traditional "ritual feast of communion." A portion of *Water* and *Salt* is removed for the "cakes"/"sweetbreads" (or "cornbread") dough. Then, *Salt* is poured into the remaining *Water* within a *Chalice*—demonstrating an "alchemical marriage" (chemical fusion) of ba-

---

hold it up to the northern direction and say, 'May the Spirits of Earth bestow their blessing and remember.'"—Joshua Free, *Elvenomicon.*

sic elements, while speaking:

> "By this alchemical expression, I do transform and purify my being unto the highest. Blessed be the alchemical change. Blessed be the Elements of Water and Earth and all that makes contact with them. Elements Unite; energies swirl. Fusion and transformation generate creation."[∞]

This *"Salted Water"* may be used to consecrate the "sacred space," *Witch's Circle* or *nemeton* area, using an *asperger*.[‡] In another tradition, the *Chalice* is taken to the north (or east) and poured out slowly, moving clockwise, around the boundary of the circle. [*Witchcraft* is best performed outdoors.]

Once its contents is mostly emptied, the *Chalice*

∞ These lines are absent in the original "Merlyn Stone" notebooks. The first part is adapted from "*Elvenomicon*" by Joshua Free; the second from "*The Druid's Handbook*" by Joshua Free. [Both volumes are contained in the Master Edition anthology: "*Merlyn's Complete Book of Druidism: A Master Course in Druidry for Modern Druids.*"]

‡ An *asperger* disperses sprinkles of water across a distance—easily constructed by attaching a pinecone to one end of a rod (or branch). Held like a wand, the pinecone end is dipped briefly into water, then drawn out and dispersed by making flicking motions in the air.

may be filled with *Wine*, because afterward, in one version of the "Great Rite" from the "*Book of Shadows*,"* the *High Priest* holds up the *Chalice* (with *Wine*) while kneeling before the *High Priestess*; and she holds the *Athame* (*Dagger*), lowering the point downward into the *Chalice*, as he says:

> "As the dagger is to male; so the chalice is to female—and joined together, they become one united truth."[4]

OF THE CAKES & WINE

The "*Book of Aradia*" provides instructions of consecration (or ingredient preparation) for "*Cakes* and *Wine*" shared by a *coven* during rituals. A tradition of basic "communion" continues in modern *Wicca* for both "*esbats*" (monthly lunar observations; i.e. *full moon*) and "*sabbats*,"

---

*   In an alternative version, the *High Priestess* (*HPS*) holds the *Chalice* between her breasts and the *High Priest* (*HP*) holds the *Athame/ Dagger*; in another modern example, both the HPS and HP share the role of holding both items together, with one's hand over the other's.

4   "HP: *Athame to Chalice*. HPS: *Spirit to Flesh*. HP: *Man to Woman*. HPS: *As the God and Goddess within*. All: *Conjoined they bring blessedness to life*."—Mary Kay Simms, *The Witch's Circle*.

referring to eight key annual holidays (seasonal festivals) of "paganism" or "neopaganism." Once the small cakes are baked, the *High Priestess* serves one to each member, saying:—

"May you never hunger."

Each member breaks a small piece off to leave in the *Offering Dish.*[†] The *Priest* fills a separate "*Communal Chalice*" to serve a sip of consecrated *Wine*[5] to each member, saying:—

"May you never thirst."

Aradian tradition indicates ingredients of the *cakes* as: *meal, salt, honey* and *water.* The "*Book of Aradia*" substitutes previously given steps (concerning *Water and Salt*) with incantations or "conjurations" directed to the *Meal* (corn meal or another grain flour) and *Salt*, followed by a "*Conjuration to Cain.*" The dough is then divided and

---

†   The intention of a true "*offering*" given up at the beginning is more significant than simply donating *leftovers*.

5   "I conjure thee, O wine! Though who at first didst grow from nothing, by light of sun and light of moon. The swelling, ripened grape; the blood of the earth pressed soon! I conjure thee, O wine! That as we drink of thee, We drink of the power of the gods; Of fire, and lightning, and rain; Of things that are wild and free!"—Ed Fitch, *Magical Rites from the Crystal Well.*

fashioned into "lunar" shapes (a *horn* or *crescent*) before baking, over which is spoken a "*Conjuration of Diana*." [Some modern traditions draw a *pentacle* (*star*) across a circular cake/cookie.] Finally, an "*Invocation to Aradia*" is employed for requests of magical power.[*]

Concerning specific recipes: they seldom appear in older grimiores.[6] Baking traditional breads, cakes and cookies—particularly using meal of a local region (*i.e. oats, corn, &tc.*)—was once a common self-sufficient knowledge, especially in more rural

---

[*]   See also the section titled: "*Role and Power of Witches.*"

[6]   The following suggestion is copied in the side-notes of Merlyn Stone's notebook: "¼ cup butter; ½ cup powdered sugar; 1 egg; 1 tsp. vanilla extract; ¼ cup milk; 1 cup ground almonds; 1 cup flour; 1 tsp. baking powder; ¼ tsp. salt. Preheat oven to 350 degrees. Grease cookie sheet. Cream butter and sugar. Add egg and vanilla, beat well. Add milk. Stir in ground almonds. Sift flour, baking soda and salt together. Beat these ingredients in to the butter mixture. The dough may be stiff; gently knead it on a floured board four or five times and then roll out the dough. Cut into crescent shapes or full moon shapes. Bake 8-10 minutes, until very lightly browned. Yield: 15-24 cakes."—Yasmine Galenorn, *Embracing the Moon.*

communities where "folk traditions" survived.[∫]
From the recension delivered by Charles Leland
(*in 1899*), the original "conjurations" and "invocations" are as follows:—

Conjuration of the Meal

I conjure thee, O Meal!
Who are indeed our body, since without you
We could not live, you who—at first as seed—
Before becoming flower, went in the earth,
Where all deep secrets hide, and then when
    ground[∞]
Did it dance like dust in the wind, and yet
    meanwhile
Did it bear with thee in flitting, strange secrets!

[∫] Another side-note regarding 'Crescent Cakes'
quotes: "This is the best recipe I've been able to
find. Most of the other published ones taste foul
—1 cup finely ground almonds; 1¼ cups flour; ½
cup confectioner's sugar; 2 drops almond extract;
½ cup softened butter; 1 egg yolk. Combine
almonds, flour, sugar, and extract until
thoroughly mixed. With the hands, work in the
butter and egg yolk until fully blended. Chill
dough. Preheat oven to 325 degrees. Pinch off
pieces of dough about the size of walnuts and
shape into crescents. Place on greased sheets and
bake for about 20 minutes." Scott Cunningham,
Wicca: A Guide for the Solitary Practitioner.

[∞] As "*flour.*"

Yet all the while, when thou were in the ear,
Even as a (golden) glittering grain, even then
The fireflies came to cast their light on you
And aid your growth, because without their
  help
You could not grow nor become beautiful;
Therefore though does belong unto the race
Of witches or fairies, and because
Fireflies do belong to the sun…

Queen of the Fireflies: hurry apace,[‡]
Come to me now as if running a race,
Bridle the horse as you hear me now sing!
Bridle, O bridle, the son of the king!

Come in a hurry and bring him to me!
The son of the king will ever set you free;
And because you are forever brilliant and fair,
Under a glass I will keep thee; while there,
With a lens I will study your secrets concealed,
'Til all their bright mysteries are fully revealed.
Yes, all the wondrous lore perplexed
Of this life to bear and of the next.
Thus to all mysteries I shall attain,
Yes, even to that, at last, of the grain;
And when this at last I shall truly know,
Firefly, freely I'll let thee go!
When Earth's dark secrets are known to me,
My blessing at last I will give to thee!

---

‡ This portion of the incantation involving the
   presence of a firefly may have originally denoted
   a subordinate ritual.

Conjuration of the Salt

I do conjure thee, Salt, lo! here at (noon),
Exactly in the middle of a stream
I take my place and see the water round,
Likewise the sun, and think of nothing else
While here, besides the Water and the Sun:
For all my soul is turned in truth to them;
Indeed, I do desire no other thought,
I yearn to learn the very truth of truths,
For I have suffered long with the desire
To know my future or my coming fate,
If good or evil will prevail in it.
Water and Sun, be gracious to me!

Conjuration to Cain

I conjure thee, O Cain, as you can never
Have rest or peace until you shall be freed
From the (sun)‡ where you are imprisoned,
   and must go
Rubbing thy hands and running about quickly:*
I pray thee let me know my destiny;
And if it is evil, change its course for me!
If you will grant this grace, I'll see it clear
In the water, in the splendor of the sun;
And you, O Cain, shall tell by word of mouth

---

‡ The "planet" or "sun" denoted here is actually
   The Moon (*Luna*).
* Alluding to attempts to "keep warm" on the cold
   Moon.

this, whatever my destiny is to be.
And unless you grant me this,
May you never know peace or bliss![∫]

Conjuration to Diana

[*The Witch puts the cakes to bake, then says:*]
I do not bake the Bread, nor with it, Salt,
Nor do I cook the Honey with the (Wine);
I bake the body and the blood and soul,
The soul of (great) Diana, that she shall
Know neither rest nor peace, and ever be
In cruel suffering until she will grant
What I request, what I do most desire,
I beg it of her from my very heart!
And if the grace be granted, O Diana!—
In honor of thee, I will hold this feast,
Feast and drain the goblet deep,
We will dance and wildly leap,
And if you so grant the grace I require,
Then when the dance is wildest, all the lamps
Shall be extinguished and we will freely love![∞]

∫ Prevalent practice of threatening "intermediary
spirits" appears increasingly throughout the
Middle Ages and particularly among *Solomonic*-
style grimoires.

∞ In many "Aradian/Dianic" and "Gardnerian"
traditions, "men and women" of the *Coven* feast
together *naked* ("*skyclad*") before celebrating
with music and dance; after which, once firelight
has dimmed, couples share sexual congress as an

Invocation to Aradia

Aradia! O my Aradia!
You who are the daughter of him—
Most evil of all spirits, who of old
Once reigned in hell when driven away from
    heaven,
Who by his sister were you sired,
But as your mother did repent her fault,
She wished to mate you to a spirit who
Should be benevolent,
And not malevolent.

Aradia, Aradia! I implore you,
By the love which Diana did bear for thee!
And by the love which I too feel for thee!
I pray you grant the grace which I require!
And if this grace be granted, may there be
One of three signs distinctly clear to me:
    —the hiss of a serpent;
    —the light of a firefly; or
    —the sound of a frog!
But if you do refuse this favor, then
May you have no future peace or joy,
And be obliged to seek me from afar,
Until you come to grant me my desire,
In haste, and then you may return again
Unto your destination. And so it is!

_____

extension of the "Great Rite."

OF THE HOLED-STONE &
PENTACLE

Chapter IV of the "*Book of Aradia*" is dedicated to
consecration of sacred stones (to *Diana*)—applied
when a *Witch* discovers either one of two types: a
"holed-stone" or "holey-stone" (which may be
seen through; corded and hung around the neck);
and/or a flat round "disc-like" stone (upon which
one could trace out a five-pointed star) appropriate
as a *focal* tool—called a "*Pentacle*" in modern
rituals. The *Witch* is instructed to hold the "holey
stone" in the air while speaking an incantation; the
round stone is to be thrown up and caught three
times "with eyes raised to heaven."*

Invocation of the Holey-Stone

I have found a holey-stone upon the ground.
O Fate! I thank you for this happy find,
Also the spirit who upon this road
Has given it to me;
And may it prove to be for my true good
And my good fortune!

I rise in the morning by the earliest dawn,†

---

* Yes, we would hope that if you *are* throwing a
  rock up in the air to catch that you *would* be
  looking skyward...

† This portion of the incantation seems to present a
  subsequent related ritual consecration of the
  talisman (or a separate amulet blessing) that

And I go forth to walk through (pleasant)
    vales,
All in the mountains or the meadows fair,
Seeking for luck while onward still I roam,
Seeking for *rue* and *vervain* scented sweet,
Because they bring good fortune unto all.
I keep them safely guarded in my bosom,[‡]
That none may know it—it is a secret thing,
And sacred too, and thus I speak the spell:
'*Vervain*, ever be a benefit,
And may thy blessing be upon the witch
Or on the fairy who did give thee to me!'

It was *Diana* who did come to me,
All in the night in a dream, and said to me:
'If you would keep all evil folk afar,
Then ever keep the *vervain* and the *rue*
Safely beside thee!'

Great *Diana*! You
Who are the queen of heaven and of earth,
And of the infernal lands—yes, you who are
Protectress of all unfortunate men,
Of thieves and murderers, and of women too
Who lead an evil life, and yet has known
That their nature was not evil; you, *Diana*,
Has still conferred on them some joy in life.

---

involves (the herbs) *vervain* and *rue*.

[‡] Alternatively for *Priests*, "Around my neck" or
"At my chest/breast" *&tc*. denoting use of the
holed-stone as a necklace.

Or I may truly at another time
So conjure thee that you shall have no peace
Or happiness, for you shall ever be
In suffering until you grant that
Which I require in strictest faith from thee!

Conjuration of the Round Stone[*]

Spirit of Good Omen,
Who has come to aid me,
Believe I had great need of thee.
Spirit of the Red Goblin,
Since you have come to aid me in my need,
I pray of thee 'do not abandon me':
I beg of thee to enter now into this stone,
That in my pocket I may carry thee,
And so when anything is needed by me,
I can call unto thee: be what it may,
Do not abandon me, by night or by day.

Should I lend money unto any man
Who will not pay when due, I pray of thee,
Red Goblin, make them pay their debt!
And if they will not and is obstinate,
Go at them with your cry of *'Bree! Bree!'*
And if they sleep, awake 'em with a twitch,
And pull the covering off and frighten 'em!
And follow them about wherever they go.
So teach them good with your ceaseless *'Bree!*

---

[*] This incantation/ritual does not mention *Diana*,
Aradia, &tc.

Bree!'
That: 'He who obligation ever forgets
Shall be in trouble until he pays his debts.'
O my Red Goblin, come unto my aid!

Or, should I quarrel with her whom I love,[∞]
Then Spirit of Good Luck, I pray you go
To her while sleeping—pull her by the hair,
And carry her through the night unto my bed!
And in the morning, when all spirits go
To their repose, shall you, when you return
Into thy stone, carry her home again,
And leave her there asleep.
Therefore, O Sprite!
I beg thee, in this stone make thy home!
Obey in every way all that I command.
So in my pocket, you shall ever be,
And you and I will never part company!

Having considered these two previous examples
from the *Aradia* book, the origins for these following instructions for the "Holy Stone Talisman"
should be well understood—as given, for example,
in *The Grimoire of Lady Sheba* (1972), where the
following "chant" (and action) is undertaken in a
field or park before "12 o'clock" on the "first day
of May" (Beltane). The being referred to above as

∞ Gender is supplied here verbatim from "*Book of
   Aradia*" as the original author/poet intended for
   its audience; implications of which we will leave
   up to the reader to consider.

the "Red Goblin" is evoked and the stone with a natural hole in it (when found) is covered in red silk.

"Walked I forth on May Day Morning,
Search I faithful, for the Round Stone.
Ask I help of Great Diana,
Ask I help of Great Arida,‡
Found I the Round Stone.
Held within my hands, the Golden Round
   Stone.
Lo, I cast my eyes toward Heaven,
Then tossed I the Round Stone toward the
   heavens; thrice
I tossed the Stone toward Heaven,
Caught I the Round Stone,
Held I fast the Round Stone,
Lest the falling Round Stone
Return to Earth, from whence I took it.

I conjure thee Red Goblin:
I conjure thee by Diana,
I conjure thee by Aradia,
Beautiful and Beloved Mother,
Lovely Goddess of all Witches,
Lovely Goddess of all Earthlings,
By them did I conjure thee.
By the word of my Moon Mother,
Lovely Goddess of the Moonbeams,
By them did I conjure thee.

---

‡   Spelled as given in the text; obviously "Aradia."

Now I pray thee, Red Goblin,
Do not abandon, or forsaken me,
For I have great need of thee.
Covered I the round stone,
With silk of red I wrapped it,
Prepared for thee a warm abode.
Rest thou inside my pocked,
Until I have need of thee.
Be thou willing to assist me,
For thou shalt do my bidding
When I call thee forth, Red Goblin.
Reside now within the Round Stone,
Until the day, when by Diana,
I release thee, to return to the Nether,
From the place whence I called thee.
So mote it be."

OF THE AIR & FIRE

Censers generating incense smoke and beacon-lamps (or candles) are basic ceremonial represent-ations of the *Air* and *Fire* elements. Traditionally, once *Salt* and *Water* are consecrated at the start of a ritual, next steps include lighting the burner (of-ten charcoal) and consecrating the *Incense* (the *Air* element). As like the *Salt* (*Earth*) and *Water* mixed together, an "alchemical change" (transformation) occurs when introducing *Incense* to *Burner*. And similarly, the result (smoke) from this fusion is used to consecrate objects (and spaces) with the

blessings of *Air* and *Fire*. A variation of the incantation from "Of the Water & Salt" (section) is
usually applied.[7]

OF ELEMENTAL & RITUAL TOOLS

Some traditions apply *more* "ceremonialism" to
the "consecration" of "ritual tools" than others.
The purpose of such rites is for the *Witch* or *Wizard*—*Priestess* or *Priest*—to apply Self-determined attention very deliberately to all objects,
actions and vocal expressions (incantations, *&tc.*)
present during ritual. For some, acts of "recognition" and "thanksgiving" simultaneous with disco-

---

7 "Hold your hands over the incense and burner,
   and say: 'I ask the Air Spirits to come and bless
   this incense. I ask the Fire Spirits to come and
   bless this burner. [In the names of … and …]
   Blessed be the Elements of Air and Fire and all
   that makes contact with them."—Joshua Free,
   Druid's Handbook. "Take the incense and hold it
   up to the east, saying: 'May the Spirits of Air
   bestow their blessing and remember.' Hold up the
   burner to the south and say: 'May the Spirits of
   Fire bestow their blessing and remember.' Add
   some incense resin to the coals (or light the stick
   you are using) and affirm: 'By this alchemical
   expression do I transform and purify my being;
   stripping away old skin, leaving my mortal
   body.'"—Joshua Free, *Elvenomicon.*

very (or construction) of a magical item is enough —on the basis that the object will receive an increased "charge" of intention (energy) during ritual operations.

Within *Witchcraft* tradition: whether a magical tool is exclusively "consecrated" in a formal ceremony or simply "charged" by repeated ritual appearances, it maintains a status of "enchanted" thereafter (by consideration of the *Witch* or practitioner); cumulative consecrations are not necessary. The basic "elemental tools"—*Pentacle Stone*, *Athame/Dagger*, *Wand* and *Chalice*—are always present and therefore actively charged from the *Witch's Circle* (again, by consideration).

There are special cases of heavy concentrated/focused energy on an object, such as the creation of a "magickal artifact," "talisman" or an appropriated vessel to "house a spirit." However, these are all particular *applications* of "ritual magic" (or "magick"), which is performed within an already consecrated *Witch's Circle*, while surrounded by (and often including use of) previously "charged" or "consecrated" ritual tools. For this reason, a *Witch* emphasizes prerequisite (preparatory) ritual work and construction or discovery of tools (in addition to theory and history) during preliminary levels ("grades" or "degrees") of initiation prior to incorporating the lot of it into further applications of "directed intention" (otherwise referred to as "spells," "spellwork" or "spellcraft") from traditional lore. Knowingness and the ability to "construct" and "consecrate" tools (energy-matter) and space(-time) naturally should come first. From the *Gardnerian Book of Shadows*:—

> "There are no magical supply shops,[∞] so unless you are lucky enough to be given or sold tools, a poor witch must extemporize. But when made, you should be able to borrow or obtain an Athame. So having made a circle, erect an Altar. Any small table or chest will do. There must be fire on it (a candle will suffice) and your book. For good results, incense is best if you can get it, but coals in a chafing dish burning sweet-smelling herbs will do. A cup, if you would have cakes and wine, and a platter with the signs drawn into the same in ink, showing a pentacle. Get a white-hilted knife and a wand (a sword is not necessary). Cut the marks with the Athame. Purify everything, then consecrate your tools in proper form and ever be properly prepared. But ever remember, magical operations are useless unless the mind can be brought to the proper attitude—keyed to

---

∞   Gerald Gardner is writing prior to repeal of Witchcraft laws in England (1951); before the rise of New Age marketplaces.

the utmost pitch.

"Affirmations must be made clearly, and the mind should be inflamed with desire. With this frenzy of will, you may do as much with simple tools as with the most complete set. But good and especially ancient tools have their own aura. They do help to bring about that reverential spirit, the desire to learn and develop your powers. For this reason, witches ever try to obtain tools from sorcerers, who being skilled men, make good tools and consecrate them well, giving them mighty power. But a great witch's tools also gain much power; and you should ever strive to make any tools you manufacture of the finest materials you can obtain, to the end that they may absorb your power the more easily. And of course, if you may inherit or obtain another witch's tools, power will flow from them."

Many have assumed that there is some hidden long-running unbroken archaic literary record of *Wiccan* rites and ceremonies, but the standards observed today are, perhaps, a century old at best.[*]

---

[*] Slightly longer now: the author is originally writing this document in 1999. Samuel MacGregor Mathers (a founding member of the *Golden Dawn*) translated the *Key of Solomon* to

Apart from minimal folklore provided in "*Book of Aradia,*" the primary source behind "consecration of ritual tools" found in the *Gardnerian Book of Shadows* is the "*Key of Solomon*" and other *kabbalistic* lore borrowed from the "*Hermetic Order of the Golden Dawn*" and the "*Ordo Templi Orientis*" (OTO).‡ In fact, Aleister Crowley contributed significantly to Gerald Gardner's original presentation of *Wicca*, prior to revisions of the *Book of Shadows* by Doreen Valiente during the 1950's and 1960's, when even more "Hebrew names" (from *Kabbalah*, etc.) and facets of "ceremonial magic" were removed.

The most efficient way to "communicate increased power"[8]—or "consecrate" an item in ritual—is to bring it into contact with manifestations previously considered "sacred." For example, the sequence observed in (previous) rites often begins with consecration of basic elements—such as *Salt* and *Water* or the *Incense* and *Burner*—which are then

---

English in 1888 from manuscripts in the British Museum. Public "anti-witchcraft laws" were not repealed in England until 1951.

‡ Henry C. Agrippa's "*Occult Philosophy*" (*4 vols.*) is another commonly consulted reference for early ritual and ceremonial magic, along with a simplified plagiarized extrapolation of the same, titled: *The Magus.*

8 Referring to a phrase used in Gerald Gardner's "*High Magic's Aid.*"

used to consecrate other objects or spaces. The next example given—the *Pentacle Stone*—is also significant here, because once consecrated by the elements, it too becomes a focal device for "charging" other objects placed upon it later. [This is particularly important when a *Witch* is just starting out; when they do not yet have consecrated tools in which to consecrate more tools.]

OF THE SWORD & DAGGER

The *Key of Solomon* describes a "white-hilt knife" consecrated for use in all magical practices except drawing (casting) of the ritual circle, which is performed with a "black-hilt knife,"[†] or what Gerald Gardner referred to as the *Athame*. Sigils and symbols carved (or painted) onto the handle for the *Book of Shadows* are exactly as they appear in the *Key of Solomon*. As objects representative of the Fire element, operations for consecrating an *Athame* are identical to a *Sword*.

According to original instructions from *Solomonic grimoires*: the white knife (and/or ceremonial sword) is constructed/consecrated "in the day and

---

† The associated use of "blood" (and other diabolical) operations from the *Key of Solomon* (and similar *grimoires*) is entirely unnecessary and included only to keep the uninitiated from successfully employing the magic.

hour of Mercury,[∞] and when Mars is in the Sign of the Ram [*Aries*] or of the Scorpion [*Scorpio*]." The black-hilt knife or *Athame* (used for "making the Circle, wherewith to strike terror and fear into spirits") is crafted "in the day and hour of Saturn."*

The blade is sprinkled with consecrated *Salt-Water* and then passed through the *Incense/Smoke* and then set on the *Pentacle* or *Stone*. An incantation for blade-consecration is given in the *Book of Shadows* as derived from the *Key of Solomon*—except only the first three "Hermetic" names from the *Key* are invoked, the "Tetragrammaton" (YH-VH) is removed and all Hebrew Divine Names are replaced with *Aradia* and *Cernunnos*.

> "I conjure thee, O [*Sword, Athame, &tc.*], by the Names—*Abrahach, Abrach, Abracadabra*—that you serve me as a strength and defense in all magical operations against all my enemies, visible and invisible. I conjure thee anew by the Holy Name *Aradia* and the Holy Name *Cernunnos*. I

∞ The first, eighth, fifteenth or twenty-second hour of Wednesday. Some begin the count at dawn; others right after midnight of the preceding day. Another tradition observes the start of a new day at the dusk of a previous.

* The same as the previous note (∞) but for Saturday.

conjure thee, O [*Sword, Athame, &tc.*], that you serve me as a protection in all adversities; so aid me now!"[9]

The blade is sprinkled and passed through the smoke a second time, giving the following prayer (which may be varied for consecrating other ritual tools):

"I conjure thee, O [*Sword, Athame, &tc.*] of Steel, by the Great Gods and Gentle Goddesses, by the virtue of the heavens, of the stars and of the spirits who preside over them, that you may receive such virtue that

---

9   "I conjure thee, O Sword, by these Names, *Abrahach, Abrach, Abracadabra, Yod He Vau He,* that thou serve me for a strength and defense in all Magical Operations, against all mine Enemies, visible and invisible. I conjure thee anew by the Holy and Indivisible Name of *El* strong and wonderful; by the name *Shaddai* almighty; and by these Names *Qadosch, Qadosch, Qadosch, Adonai Elohim Tzabaoth, Emanuel,* the First and the Last, Wisdom Way, Life, Truth, Chief, Speech, Word, Splendor, Light, Sun, Fountain, Glory, the Stone of the Wise, Virtue, Shepherd, Priest, Messiah Immortal; by these Names then, and by the other Names, I conjure thee, O Sword, that thou servest me for a Protection in all adversities. Amen."—trans. S.L. MacGregor Mathers, *Key of Solomon.*

I may obtain the end that I desire in all things wherein I shall use thee, by the power of *Aradia* and *Cernunnos.*"[10]

OF THE WAND & STAFF

The *Key of Solomon*[11] instructs that the *Staff* should be constructed of *elderwood*, or *cane* or *rosewood*; and the *Wand* of *hazel* or *nut* tree. The wood being *virgin*,[12] meaning "of one year's

---

10 "*Asophiel, Asophiel, Asophiel, Pentagrammaton, Athanatos, Eheieh Asher Eheieh, Qadosch, Qadosch, Qadosch*; O God Eternal, and my Father, bless this Instrument prepared in Thine honor, so that it may only serve for a good use and end, for Thy Glory. Amen."—trans. S.L. MacGregor Mathers, *Key of Solomon.* This basic prayer, excluding the Hebrew names, appears in the *Book of Shadows* for consecrating other ritual tools.

11 "*Adonai*, Most Holy, deign to bless and consecrate this Wand, and this Staff, that they may obtain the necessary virtue, through Thee, O Most Holy *Adonai*, Whose kindgom endures unto the Ages of the Ages. Amen."—trans. S.L. MacGregor Mathers, *Key of Solomon.*

12 "...grimoires seem to have differing opinions of *virgin wood.* In one description, the wand comes from a branch that has no other shoots; in another, the tree must be less than a year old or

growth only" and cut from the tree in a single stroke, "on the day of Mercury, at sunrise."[‡] Where an *Athame* often substitutes the *Sword* of "ceremonial magic," the *Wand* may serve in place of a *Staff*; in some traditions, a *Staff* can also substitute symbolism of a *Sword*.

Witches often prefer *Wands* of *hazel* or *willow*; considerably more details regarding tree/wood types and corresponding energies may be found in Druid lore.[†] Some archaic sources suggest a 21-inch long *Wand*, although 12-to-18 inches is more workable length. A popular guide-rule is the "length of your elbow to your fingertips. Another *Wiccan* tradition describes removing two limbs from a *Willow* tree at night during a *full moon*: the *Wand* is 13-inches long and a companion *Staff* is 39-inches. The *Witch* then treats the wood several

---

not yet having bared any fruit."—Joshua Free, *The Great Magickal Arcanum: A Master Course in Magick for Modern Wizards.*

[‡] Wednesday is the "Day of Mercury"— by some counts of planetary hours, *sunrise on a Wednesday* is also the "Hour of Mercury."

[†] Refer to "*Elvenomicon -or- Secret Traditions of Elves and Faeries: The Book of Elven Magick & Druid Lore*" by Joshua Free; also found in the Master Edition anthology: "*Merlyn's Complete Book of Druidism: A Master Course in Druidry for Modern Druids.*"

times with a *chamomile* tincture.[13]

Although often simplified and bastardized from their true sources, many elements of other *Solomonic-cycle* "*grimoires*" frequently appeared in *Wicca* during the 20th century. One example, found in a popular *Witchcraft* tome from the 1970's, actually incorporates construction of a "*Blasting Rod*"[*] exactly as suggested in a diabolical sorcerer's handbook known as the "*Grand Grimoire*"[∞] as given below, paraphrasing the origi-

---

13 "Another method of preparing a Magic Rod ordains that it shall be a branch of the hazel-tree born during the year of operation. It must be cut on the first Wednesday after the new moon, between 11 P.M. and midnight. The knife must be new and the branch severed by a downward stroke. The rod must then be blessed; at the stouter end must be written the word AGLA †, in the center ON †, and towards the point TETRAGRAMMATON †. Lastly say over it: *Conjuro te cito mihi obedire—I conjure thee to obey me forthwith.*"—A.E. Waite, *The Complete Book of Ceremonial Magic.*

* Traditionally used by sorcerers to threaten spirits that do not arrive when evoked, or attack entities that do not submit to the magician's bidding.

∞ Medieval grimoires of "kabbalistic sorcery" include not only the *Key of Solomon the King*, and it's *Lesser Key: The Goetia*, but also the *Grand Grimoire (Red Dragon)*, *Grimoirum*

nal source text described by Arthur Edward Waite (*in 1911*):—

> *"The 'Grand Grimoire' devotes an entire chapter to the true composition of the Mysterious Wand, otherwise the Destroying or Blasting Rod. It mentions no other instrument, and ascribes to it all the power in diabolical evocations... On the eve of the great enterprise, says this Ritual, you must go in search of a wand or rod of wild hazel which has never borne fruit; its length should be nineteen and a half inches. When you have met with a wand of the required form, touch it only with your eyes; let it stay until the next morning, which is the day of operation. Then you must cut it absolutely at the moment when the sun rises; strip it of its leaves and lesser branches, if there be any, using your ritual blade or knife...*
>
> *"Having pronounced the incantation[14] and*

Verum and *Grimoire of Honorius (Black Dragon)*. Interest in other popular grimoires— *The Sacred Book of Magic of Abramelin the Mage, the Enchiridion,&tc.*—also increased at the end of the 19th century, and continuing during public revival of the *Craft*.

14 "Begin cutting it when the sun is first rising over the hemisphere and pronounce the following

still keeping your eyes turned towards the region of the rising sun, you may finish cutting your rod, and may then carry it to your abode. You must next go in search of a piece of ordinary wood, fashion the two ends like those of the genuine rod and take it an ironsmith to weld two pointed caps that will affix to said ends. This done, you may again return home, and there, with your own hands, affix the steel caps to the genuine rod. Subsequently, you must obtain a lodestone and magnetize the steel ends, pronouncing the second incantation."[15]

---

words: 'I beseech Thee, O Grand *Adonay*, *Eloim*, *Ariel*, and *Jehovam*, to be propitious unto me, and to endow this Wand, which I am cutting, with the power and virtue of the rods of *Jacob*, of *Moses*, and of the mighty *Joshua!* I also beseech Thee, O Grand *Adonay*, *Eloim*, *Ariel*, and *Jehovam*, to infuse into this Rod the whole strength of *Samson*, the righteous wrath of *Emanuel* and the thunders of mighty *Zariatnatmik*, who will avenge the crimes of men at the Day of Judgment! Amen."—*Grand Grimoire.*

15 "By the Grand *Adonay*, *Eloim*, *Ariel*, and *Jehovam*, I bid thee join with and attract all substances which I desire. By the power of the sublime *Adonay*, *Eloim*, *Ariel*, and *Jehovam*, I command thee, by the opposition of fire and water, to separate all substances, as they were separated on the day of the world's creation.

A SUMMARY OF RITUAL TOOLS[‡]

The *Cup* or *Chalice* holds drinkable liquids: water, wine, ceremonial mead and other ritual libations. It naturally represents the *Water* element and is placed in the *west* during rituals. A *Cauldron* is simply another version of the *Cup*, used for brewing fusions, potions and tinctures—and likewise makes stereotypical appearances in *Witchcraft.* Alcohol may also be burned within it.

Pentacles symbolize the *Earth* element and come in a variety of styles and sizes—from circular plates of wood, metal, wax or clay, to the traditional stones—used as a focal point of the *Altar*, which is placed in the *northern* quadrant of the working area. The tool is so named for the five-pointed star engraved or drawn across its surface.

The *Magic Blade*—a *Dagger/Athame* or *Sword*—symbolizes a *Witch's* sheer cutting will (and the force or desire necessary for traditional magic) and representative of the *Fire* element (and thus placed in the *south* during ritual). Herbalists will also keep a separate knife used only for cutting plants and herbs.

The *Wand* represents the *Air* element in ritual and

Amen."—*Grand Grimoire.*

[‡] Paraphrased from the text of the *"Sorcerer's Handbook."*

the action that is transmitted in thought. In folk traditions and *Witchcraft*, they are often made of wood—such as *Hazel* or *Willow*. Other tree associations include *Apple* for love, *Ash* for healing, *Pine* for prosperity, *Rowan* for protection and *Birch* for purification. A *Wand* averages about fifteen to eighteen inches long and half an inch thick. They are placed in the *east* during rituals.

THE WITCH'S CIRCLE
(Merlyn Stone, Autumn '98)

Here we discuss the *"Witch's Circle"* or *Magic Circle* of the Arts, where all "ritual magic" (or *magick*) is performed. Each tradition and *grimoire* suggests its unique style and methodology behind "creation of sacred space" or "temple erection."

Originally, the *Craft* of *Witches* was practiced and disseminated in rural areas by folk with little access to national temples, ceremonial chambers and elaborate (and often expensive) tools maintained by the *Priests* and *Priestesses* practicing magic *within* the system and urban domain (or "realm") of ancient magical cultures (and their religions). This accounts for the various differences in carrying out physical practices of *"paganism"* and *"magick."*

Sources of "magical lore" and "ritual texts" for *Witchcraft* were often imported by preexisting members of larger (and nationally sanctioned) organizations—*Orders*, *Lodges*, *Guilds* and *Temples.*

We then see—starting in ancient Mesopotamia—a clear dividing line (regarding social class) between those practicing magic *within* the "system" (acting as "religio-government" officials, *&tc.*) of historic *Temples* in urbanized society, versus those operating independently on the "outskirts" of said social order; and which were able to bring various elements from the sanctioned "Ancient Mystery School" with them into the wilds—where they undoubtedly mirrored facsimiles of religious hierarchy, knowledge grades and initiation structures, while establishing *Witchcraft* traditions of their own design.

MAGICAL PREPARATIONS (AN APPRENTICE PRIMER)

Methods of "*casting a circle*" or conducting "*ritual magic*" are as personal and varied as interpretations of mythology, religion and "deity" can be. Contrary to styles of "ceremonial magicians"— those that operate elaborate rites indoors, within a highly decorated temple—*Witches* are accustomed to working exclusively outdoors (and in seclusion) with simpler tools and techniques. There are obvious advantages to both routes. For our present purposes, we will focus only on those "ceremonial" elements traditionally incorporated into *Wiccan* practices since the original circulation of Gerald Gardner's "*Book of Shadows*" (and other similar versions) during the 20th century.

Much like consecration of "objects" or "masses," the consecration (or "creation") of "space" is accomplished by *consideration*—meaning the Self-determined "thought" directed by a *Witch*. Basic principles applied to the *Witch's Circle* (for purposes of understanding and practicing modern *Wicca*) are generally applicable to all forms of "ritual magic," particularly where they are often borrowed from the same lore—and this reason, the two areas of esoteric study often blend as a modern "applied spiritual/metaphysical philosophy."

It is the basic principles, such as set forth in the current series of handbooks,* that renders the "magick" effective at all, regardless of the cultural flavor or mythological personality that is superimposed over it for individuality. These other religious flavors are *added* to the basics—to the benefit or detriment of the practitioner—based on one's own interests and inclinations. Of course, one of the allures of the "magical path" is that it practically demands that an individual construct their own "personal universe" in which to operate from, independent (yet connected by considerations of *Self*) to the "physical universe."

It is from a "higher" vantage point as the *True Self* —and gradients of spiritual clarity along the way —that a *Witch*, a *Mystic*, a *Magician*, *Priestess* or

---

* Referring to the original 1990's (proposed) "Merlyn Stone" trilogy—*Sorcerer's Handbook*, *Witch's Handbook* and *Druid's Handbook* (all of which are now restored and available in hardcover collector's editions).

Wizard is able to glean *any* "true knowledge" of *this* "physical universe"—and which has otherwise been considered somehow "supernatural" as an incredible misnomer.‡

Although modern *Witchcraft* rightly places an emphasis on "operative circles" (magical workings meant to invite positive change), the "occult history" reveals a long-standing tradition of *magic-users* that applied extensive efforts into fashioning "protective circles" and "blasting rods"—components of "psychic" (or "psionic") warfare with the same "forces" they are threatening for assistance. Such practitioners operate in a state of *fear* and validate the low-level consideration that properly handling energy flows is an unknown mystery.

Prior to consecration rites—or any work within the Cirlce—a *Witch's* magic begins with "purification." This is a natural integral of "magical lifestyles," but more attention is given to it immediately prior to ritual. In some ancient traditions, particular regimens and practices precede the ceremonies with a "purification bath." While this may have once been conducted in a more elaborate manner in grandiose temples, there are modernized and more personal versions observed in *Wicca*. Even apart from *'Circle Magic,'* the basic rules of intention (and, if desired, affirmation or

‡   *Misnomer*, as in: improperly named, therefore, improperly defined (and misunderstood).

incantation) may be applied to the *bath-water* and *bath-salts*. But the step is critical in any true "*priestcraft*" and even appears in the basic instructions from the "*Book of Shadows*":—

> *To practice the Art successfully, you need the following five things—one for each point of the Witch's Pentacle:*
>
> *1. Intention—You must have the absolute will to succeed, the firm belief that you can do so and the determination to win through against all obstacles.*
>
> *2. Preparation—You must be properly prepared.*
>
> *3. Invocation—The Mighty Ones must be invoked.*
>
> *4. Consecration—The Witch's Circle must be properly cast and consecrated and you must have properly consecrated tools.*
>
> *5. Purification—You must be purified.*

THE PURIFICATION BATH

Of course, purification rites, ceremonial baths and sweat-lodge traditions are not unique to the *Witch*, or the ceremonial magician. This is one instance of commonality that we respect as an underlying truth behind magical work—although frequently overlooked. Esoteric instructions, such as those suggested by *Franz Bardon*,[16] describe acts that we would today refer to as "skin and pore exfoliation." Modern *Wiccan* traditions often borrow from the *Key of Solomon*.[17] The *grimoire* explains that when a practitioner enters the waters of a "river or running stream" or a "tub in thy secret cabinet," they are to say:—

---

16 "...brush yourself with a soft natural brush until your skin becomes slightly pinkish. This will open your pores and allow them to breathe better. Through this, for the greater part, your kidneys are relieved. After this, wash your entire body with cold water, then give your body a rub-down with a rough terry towel until you feel comfortably warm. Make this procedure a daily routine and maintain it for the rest of your life..."—Franz Bardon, *Initiation Into Hermetics.*

17 "The bath often becomes a ritual itself. Candles can be burned in the bathroom, along with incense. Fragrant oils or herbal sachets can be added to the water. My favorite purification bath sachet consists of equal parts of rosemary, fennel, lavender, basil, thyme, hyssop, vervain, mint, with a touch of ground valerian root. (This formula is derived from *The Key of Solomon.*) Place this in a cloth, tie the ends up to trap the herbs inside, and pop it in the tub."—Scott Cunningham, *Wicca: A Guide for the Solitary Practitioner.*

"I conjure thee, O Creature of Water, by [the God and Goddess] who has created thee and gathered thee together into one place so that the dry land appeared, that thou uncover all the deceits of the Enemy, and that thou cast out from thee all the impurities and uncleanliness of the Spirits of the World of Phantasm, so they may harm me none, through the virtue of the Almighty [God and Goddess] who live and reign unto the Ages of the Ages. So shall it be."[∞]

Having washed clean with a preliminary bath, the *Witch* emerges (from the tub, *&tc.*) and is sprinkled with consecrated waters (infused with hyssop), saying:

"O [God and Goddess], purge me, and I shall be clean; wash me, and I shall be whiter than snow. Cast from me all impurity, that I may accomplish all things."

[∞] The additional Hermetic names repeated "twice or thrice, until thou art completely washed and clean" are: *Mertalia, Musalia, Dophalia, Onemalia, Zitanseia, Goldaphaira, Dedulsaira, Ghevialaira, Gheminaira, Gegropheira, Cedahi, Gilthar, Godieb, Ezoiil, Musil, Grassil, Tamen, Pueri, Godu, Huznoth, Astachoth, Tzabaoth, Adonai, Agla, On, El, Tetragrammaton, Shema, Aresion, Anaphaxeton, Segilaton, Primeumaton.*

Then the *Witch* shall robe; and taking up the *Bath-Salts* (or an appropriate herbal sachet) says:

> "The blessing of the Almighty [God and Goddess] be upon this Creature of Salt [*or Earth, for sachets*], and let all malignity and hindrance be cast out, and let all good enter herein."‡

And saying this, the *Witch* takes the *Bath-Salts* (or sachet) and casts it into the waters/bath, disrobes and enters to bathe a second time before adorning proper ritual garments.

RITUAL DRESSINGS & ATTIRE

A discussion of "ritual tools" and "elemental weapons" appears in another essay,* but there is still the matter of a *Witch's* dressings and garments —such as "*robes*" and "*cloaks*"—to attend to. Use of "ritual attire" is a standard practice in any *Witchcraft* tradition. The most commonly adopted color is black, especially when practicing lunar magic and other "nighttime" rituals. Some practiti-

---

‡   The additional Hermetic names are: *Imanel, Arnamon, Imato, Memeon, Rectacon, Muoboii, Paltellon, Decaion, Yamenton, Yaron, Tatonon, Vaphoron, Gardon, Existon, Zagveron, Momerton, Zarmesiton, Tileion, Tixmion.*

*   See chapter on "Rites of Consecration."

oners celebrate the "Wheel of the Year"—as festival ceremonies called "*sabbats*"—by wearing colors (or accenting with scarves) that correspond with the seasons. There are also traditions that distinguish various "degrees" or "levels" of initiation with a particular color[†] or accent—such as stripes on the cuff of a sleeve, *etc*.

To fully treat the subject of "ritual attire" for *Witchcraft*, we must also include a consideration of what may refer to as "*skyclad*"—"dressed by the sky"—which is to say *naked*. This is a traditional practice directly expressed in the *Aradian* (*Dianic*) lore and Gerald Gardner's original *Book of Shadows*.[∫] In modern times, it is generally reserved for solitary rites and close groups or "closed covens." There is also the idea of simply being naked beneath *robes* and/or *cloaks*. One recent example, observed by the current author, involved practitioners wearing only very sheer (almost see-through) black *robes*, which the *High Priestess* even left open in the front. Of course, as

---

[†] For example, in a traditional *Druid Order* —"Ovate" novitiates wear green; "Bards" wear blue; "Druids" wear white; and "High Druids" and "Arch Druids" often also wear red (and gold).

[∫] Several sources suggest strongly that, *Wicca* aside, Gerald Gardner was a naturist (nudist), which may have also played a role in the inclusion of *skyclad* practices.

a general rule, no one should ever be forced to operate outside of their comfort level.[18]

As a simplification for our purposes, we find another suggestion supplied to initiates in Ed Fitch's
Outer Court Book of Shadows, where: although it
notes that the "*Inner Court of Witchcraft*" practices "sky-clad, where the "Outer Court" (those
who have not been initiated to the "Third Degree"
or "Third Circle") is concerned, there is a "lesser
degree of Magical experience, and to maintain the
proper control, the members must wear robes." It
is further noted that "shoes and underclothes" are
not worn beneath except where weather requires.

---

18 "A good reason for skyclad working—and the
    one most quoted—is a very practical one:
    experienced opinion holds that it is easier to raise
    psychic power with an uncovered body than with
    a covered one... psychic power-raising is a two-
    sided process of input and output (increased
    awareness and increased psychic energy
    amplifying each other by mutual feedback)... the
    naked body is more responsive not only to
    sensory impressions but also to psychic ones. An
    interesting biological footnote: 'pheromones' or
    external chemical messengers... the air around us
    is full of... information which we emit and which
    we receive from others; much of it unconsciously,
    but we react to it all the time."—Janet & Stuart
    Farrar, *The Witches' Way*.

There is one additional matter to consider when one is working toward spiritual goals via the magical lifestyle: whether or not emphasis on using various "symbols" and adornment of additional "layers" is truly the route toward higher realizations of Self-actualization—or else true empowerment. The ritual aspects of "magick" and *Witchcraft* are intended as a tool, not a crutch. As a "source-point," a *Witch* intends to *create* effects with magic; not *be* the effects of their creations. Here, the Farrar's point out in *The Witches' Bible*:

> "*A final advantage to skyclad working is particularly important with some personalities; the ones who have genuine occult potential but are glamourized by the appeal of splendid robes and trappings (a by-product, of course, of the Persona problem.*"

It is true that practice of "naturism" differs greatly, by comparison, to traditions of "high magic" (of the temples) and the "ceremonial arts" observed by *Priests* and *Priestesses* on public display or even in the Orders and Lodges working from *grimoires* and other arcane magical notebooks. Even the ritual formula so often borrowed from the "*Key of Solomon*" is practiced robed (with special signs and sigils sewn thereon), after having performed the purification bath rite. It goes on to instruct:—

"The exterior garments which the Master of the Art should wear ought to be of linen, as well as those which are worn beneath; and if means allow, they should be of silk... (If they are linen, the thread of which they are made should have been spun by a young maiden.) The characters should be embroidered on the breast with the Needle of the Art° in red silk. The shoes should also be white (leather), upon which the characters should be traced in the same way. Besides this, the Master of the Art should have a Crown made of virgin paper, upon which should be four names—one on each side—written in the Pen and Ink of the Art* and marked in scarlet red. Take notice that if the linen garments were vestments of the Levites or of the Priests, and had been used for holy things, that they would be all the better."‡

∞   *"...of the Art"* meaning: "ceremonially consecrated."

*   The *Key of Solomon* uses the Hebrew names: *Yod He Vau He* in front; *Adonai* behind; *El* on the right; and *Elohim* on the left.

‡   The *Key of Solomon* suggests a prayer while dressing with the garments: "*Amor, Amator, Amides, Ideodaniach, Pamor, Plaior, Anitor;* through the merits of these holy Angels will I robe and indue myself with the Vestments of

Basic magical attire can be crafted fairly easily and inexpensively. I constructed my own first *cloak* with a few yards of bargain fabric—which is usually sold in 45-inch or 60-inch widths. There are also more involved costume patterns available at these same outlets. But even a new initiate with elementary sewing skills can make their own *robes* and *cloaks*. To close this primer, we should also distinguish between a "*robe*" and a "*cloak*" as general terms.

For our purposes: a "*robe*" generally has sleeves and is tied off at the waist—whereas a "*cloak*" often does not have sleeves and either covers an individual wearing a "*robe*" ¾ or all of the way. A ½ or ¼ *cloak* might be considered a "cape." A "*robe*" may or may not have a hood, whereas the "*cloak*" usually does. It is not uncommon to have a simple white or black robe pulled over as a one-piece and tied about the waist that is then accented by an appropriate (black) "cloak" (which is usually attached or closed at the neckline).

CASTING THE WITCH'S CIRCLE

Creating sacred space just as much concerns the

Power, through which may I conduct unto the desired end those things which I ardently wish, through Thee, O Most Holy *Adonai*, Whose Kingdom and Empire endures forever. Amen."

personal mental projection of "anchor points" in this universe as it does marking or defining the physical boundaries of a "Magic Circle." Rather than being a further *agreement* to the "reality" of *this* physical universe (as a microcosm), the Ritual Circle is actually a "macrocosm" of the personal universe or worldview directed by Self and reflected outwardly.[†] It is from within a consecrated personal workspace—whereby Self operates exterior to this physical universe—that a *Witch* directs their intentions into affecting or manifesting changes *in* the physical universe.

Rather than being a source of "protection" against the spirits and energies evoked, the "Magic Circle" can be better treated as a "portal" between worlds; or at the very least, the boundaries of a time-space. There are no dangers to evoking true magick, but there is still the matter of the "individual" themselves and their own ability to command and control magickal forces and energies—hence within a "Magic Circle" and projected "anchor points" of Self-Awareness as *focal points*, the "Mind-System" can be better brought and maintained under Self-control.

One of a *Witch's* most stereotypical icons—the

---

† See also the newly recorded audio lectures for the "*Mardukite Master Course*" by Joshua Free— esp. Volumes I and II. Transcripts also available in "*The Complete Mardukite Master Course*."

broomstick—appears frequently in modern practices of "clearing" or "purifying" the ritual space,
whereby the *Witch* literally "sweeps" the area
clean prior to any ceremony, which is a treatment
of the ground or earth.[∞] This practice—and others
for "casting a circle"—emphasizes rendering
preexisting energy *null*, while expanding Self-determined management of one's own personal
considerations of the space. Additional "purification" operations are employed any time a rite or
tradition calls for a space to be "smudged" or "in-
censed" ("*censed*")—which is a treatment of the
air. Use of incense is common in all modern
witchcraft.

A sacred circle may be physically prepared when
appropriate. It is common for *Witches* to gather in
"groves" of trees and "henges" of stones—such as
is referred to in Druidic traditions of Europe. A
small "stone circle"may be erected, either perman-
ently or temporarily. It's not uncommon to prepare
several (typically three) concentric circles (within
one another). A solitary practitioner often uses
their own height as the diameter for the inner most

∞   Update: practices involving a *broomstick* have
    dwindled in modern revivals. Once
    stereotypically aligned to "flying" (riding) or
    dancing about like a May Pole, some have
    interpreted the "broom and cauldron" motifs to be
    a bit too "cute," while other traditionalists cling
    to them as timeless icons of *witchcraft*.

circle for temporary purposes. Most "ceremonial magic" (and suggestions from *grimoires*) require much larger spaces, especially if utilized by several participants.

The following instructions are given in the "*Key of Solomon*" and are included to illustrate the most basic source of casting a *Witch's* circle available to Gerald Gardner and Aleister Crowley in the construction of the original "*Book of Shadows*."

> "*Having chosen a place...take your [sickle or scimitar] and stick into the centre of the place where the Circle is to be made; then take a cord of nine feet in length, fasten one end to the [sickle] and with the other end trace out the circumference of the Circle, which may be marked with the Sword or the [Athame]. Then, within the Circle, mark out four regions, namely, towards East, West, South and North, wherein place [symbols]; and beyond the limits of this Circle describe with the [Athame] or Sword another Circle, but leaving an open space in the North whereby you may enter and depart beyond; and beyond that you shall describe another Circle at a foot distance with the aforesaid instrument...*"

A similar operation found in Druidic lore regards use of a "*Rod*" to trace a circle—which was technically two "rods" connected by a cord. By fixing one of the ends or "rods" into the ground, the other end could be used like a geometer's "compass" to draw a circle.[19] Given that *Witchcraft* traditions were first observed in secret, any physical trace of a "Magic Circle" had to be temporary—and thus a circle would have to be marked newly with each rite. This is not always the case any more, such as when repeatedly using a site that has a more permanent boundary marked with trees or stones. In either case, ceremonially speaking, a Magic Circle is still "ritually cast" before any operations are performed, as an intentional "consecration of space."

THE FOUR QUARTERS

To the same extent that the Magic Circle is the microcosm/macrocosm of the Greater Universe, the four directions define the "ends" of the Universe —and are often called "*Watchtowers.*" The concept of the *Watchtowers* was adopted into *Wicca* via traditional dissemination of Gerald Gardner's

---

19 "The complete *Druid's Rod* is composed of three measured parts (two rods and a cord)—each 2.72 (or 3) feet in length—making the total length 9 feet (or 8.16 if strictly using the Megalithic Yard)."—Joshua Free/Merlyn Stone, *The Druid's Handbook.*

Book of Shadows. It is included within modern *Witchcraft* tradition exactly as it appears in rites of the "Hermetic Order of the Golden Dawn" (founded in 1888), of which Gerald Gardner may have been a member of, or if not, had direct access to variations used by the "Ordo Templi Orientis" (via Aleister Crowley).[20]

Ritual observance of the *Watchtowers* predates revival traditions of ceremonial magic and even Semitic Kabbalah lore (which is also frequently incorporated into *Wicca*). This concept is found in ancient Mesopotamia many thousands of years ago —particularly in rites attributed to the Babylonians and Chaldeans—and then later alluded to in the *"Chaldean Oracles of Zoroaster."* It is surprisingly curious just how little attention is given to the origins—or even the idea or subject—of the *Watch-*

---

20 "...what old Gerald told me, and on the rather disjointed state of the rituals which he had when I first knew him: they were heavily influenced by Crowley and the O.T.O., but underneath there was a lot which wasn't Crowley at all, and wasn't the Golden Dawn or ceremonial magic either— and I had been studying all three of these traditions for years. Yes, I am responsible for a lot of the wording of the present-day rituals; but not the framework of those rituals or the ideas upon which they are based."—letters from Doreen Valiente, quoted by Margot Adler in *Drawing Down The Moon.*

towers based on the widespread use of such se-
mantics throughout the rituals of the Golden Dawn
and *Wicca.*

Popular use of *Watchtowers* in modern *Wiccan*
rituals and ceremonial magic is primarily a result
of "Enochian Magic"[21]—which, combined with
the *"Kabbalah,"* served as the major cornerstone
of the late-19th century magical revival as observed by groups such as "The Hermetic Order of
the Golden Dawn," "Aurum Solis" and "Ordo
Templi Orientis" (among others)—all of which
contributed in some part to the *Book of Shadows*
on which 20th (and 21st) century *Wicca* (and other
forms of "operative neopaganism") are based...
even if acknowledgment and recognition of this
fact has since waned.

The "quarters" or "corners" of the Universe are
addressed as "opening rites" or during the "circle
casting" of all traditional ritual magic—even when
not addressed as *"Watchtowers."* For example, in
one text, it may speak of *calling* to the "Watchtower of the North" whereas another speaks of
"Guardians of the Earth Plane" (addressed toward
the northern direction)—both essentially serve the

---

21 "There are four Watchtowers and thirty Aethyrs
    with a Tablet of Union uniting all. They are
    located between the lofty realms of divinity and
    our physical Earth."—Gerald Schueler, *Enochian
    Physics.*

same function.

This concept of "addressing" or "anchoring" personal realizations of *six directions* is as ancient as magic, or at least the languages able to describe magical rites. On some of the oldest cuneiform tablet records surviving from ancient Mesopotamia—and particularly Babylon—we discover frequent mention of an *"Incantation of Eridu,"*[*] where specific names and attributes for the *four* cardinal directions are conjured in addition to *"above"* and *"below."* Thousands of years later, via the path of Kabbalistic Magic, a version of this same rite (very closely approximating the original) is among the most popular workings used by the Golden Dawn—*and* even early traditions of *Wicca* —known as the L.B.R.P. or *Lesser Banishing Ritual of the Pentagram.*

In ceremonial magic operations, banners may be hung in each direction and/or correlating "elemental tablets"—or representative objects—are similarly placed at the boundary of the ritual circle. Some grimoires recommend use of beacons or candle-lit lamps, appropriately arranged, to signify the four quarters. In traditional *Witchcraft*, a single candle (of corresponding elemental color) is set out at each cardinal point. These are lit in turn, as the "Guardians" of each *Watchtower* (or "Elem-

---

* Also referred to as the *Incantation of the Deep* (or *Enki*).

ental Realm") are conjured during the initial "casting" of the Magic Circle.

ELEMENTAL CANDLE SUGGESTIONS[‡]
North—Earth—Green (or Brown)
East—Air—Yellow (or Purple)
South—Fire—Red (or Orange)
West—West—Blue (or Grey)

"Circle-casting" rites from various *Wiccan Book of Shadows*, and other ceremonial magic sources, instruct use of an *Athame* (magic dagger) to *trace* the Magic Circle (and any of its "signs"), whereas another variation uses a *Wand*. [By this we mean, "mental" or "astral" *tracing*; not the physical boundary, which would have been marked out already.] Another variation suggests strongly that the Circle is *traced* and *consecrated* with each of the elements—meaning also "clockwise" or "sunwise" movement around the boundary of the Circle, for example, with *incense*, the *salt-water* fusion, marked by a *blade* and traced with a *Wand*.

"Elemental" or "directional" orientation of a ritual is typically indicated in texts, however this is not always the case. Some rites are written with an assumption that the *Witch* already operates within a

---

[‡] Original elemental color suggestions from *Sorcerer's Handbook*—Earth, green/black (white); Air, yellow (purple); Fire, red (green); Water, blue (orange).

particular tradition regarding this—but as with many aspects of *Witchcraft*, there are differing practices (instructed or suggested) in various sources. The traditional modern standard is to orient/align altars, and make the first address to the elements, in the eastern direction; others strongly encourage north—I've often split the difference by setting the altar to face the northeast.[†]

The *Witch* goes to the eastern point of the Magic Circle[∞] and lights the elemental candle for Air,[*] saying:

"Hail to the Guardians of the Watchtower

[†] Of course, when addressing visible planets, a *Witch* operating in the United States will note that the "celestial arc" or horizon line where all planets stream across the sky is southerly, arcing from a line of sight in the east to the south and over to the west.

[∞] This text is written with the solitary practitioner as a consideration. In another variation, a particular member of the *coven* is "stationed" at each representative quarter to address that element; and another suggests that members of the *coven* each move together around the Magic Circle to each "station."

[*] Some modern *Wicca-Witchcraft* traditions continue to supplement this rite with "tracing a pentagram in the air" from the Golden Dawn "*L.B.R.P.*" (see *The Sorcerer's Handbook*).

of the East, Spirits of Air; I summon and stir thee, Powers of Wind; I call thee forth to witness this rite and guard this Magic Circle."[22]

And in the South:

"Hail to the Guardians of the Watchtower of the South, Spirits of Fire; I summon and stir thee, Powers of Flame; I call thee forth to witness this rite and guard this Magic Circle."

And in the West:

"Hail to the Guardians of the Watchtower of the West, Spirits of Water; I summon and stir thee, Powers of Sea; I call thee forth to witness this rite and guard this Magic Circle."

---

22 In ceremonial magic, various archaic names are intoned and then, "By the Names and Letters of the Eastern Quadrangle, I invoke thee Spirits of the Watchtower of the East." Alternatively from the *Book of Shadows*—"Ye Lords of the Watchtowers of the East, ye Lords of Air; I do summon, stir and call you up, to witness our rites and to guard the Circle." Alternatively from *The Witch's Circle*—"Guardian of the Eastern Sphere, now we seek your presence here. Come, East, come. Be here this night. [*Bell rung three times.*] All hail the Watchtower of the East."

And in the North:

> "Hail to the Guardians of the Watchtower of the North, Spirits of Earth; I summon and stir thee, Powers of Stone; I call thee forth to witness this rite and guard this Magic Circle."

This being completed, the *Witch* completes their pass around the circle back to the east, then returns to the altar to commence the remainder of the ritual.

THE WITCHES' RUNE & CHANT

After Doreen Valiente worked with Gerald Gardner to revise his *Book of Shadows*, a particular incantation began appearing in future versions of the "Opening Rites" of *Wicca* through the 1970's.[‡] A version of it also appears in Gerald Gardner's novel: *High Magic's Aid*. Lines containing "Arida"/ "Aradia" and "Kernunnos"/"Cernunnos" were later added to the archaic version. These may be replaced by different ones for a patron "Goddess" and "God" of personal choice. This chant also employs two other names of unknown significance, named "Azarak" and "Zomelak."

[‡] For example, it appears in Farrar's *Witches' Bible* (1981, 1984) and *The Grimoire of Lady Sheba* (1972, 1974).

According to available research, the "*Eko, Eko*" lines (employing deity names) were absorbed into the "Witches' Rune" from from older sources,[23] which are also used in the *Book of Shadows*—the full text of which has since been equated (perhaps inaccurately) to a "rallying" for the Samhain (Halloween) festival—although it appears commonly in every standard rite.[24] This rite is essentially a

---

23 The "*Eko Eko*" lines were first published in in the 1921 issue of *Form* (an art periodical published by ceremonial magician and mystic, Austin Osman Spare); reprinted later in *The Occult Review* (April 1926). The words were originally provided (without any additional explanation) by Major General J.F.C. Fuller, a British officer, occultist, historian and apprentice of Aleister Crowley. *Eko! Eko! Azarak! Eko! Eko! Zomelak! Zod-ru-koz e Zod-ru-koo, Zod-ru-goz e Goo-ru-moo! Eko! Eko! Hoo! Hoo! Hoo!*

24 The remainder of the text may be found in the French play written by Jean Bodel in 1261 titled: *Le Miracle de Théophile* (The Miracle of Theophilus)—in which it is used by a Sorcerer to "invoke the devil": *Bagahi laca bachahé, Lamac cahi achabahé, Karrelyos. Lamac, lamec bachalyos, Cabahagi sabalyos, Baryolas. Lagozatha cabyolas, Samahac et famyolas, Harrahya.* Interestingly, another French play by Bodel (titled *Le Jeu de saint Nicolas*) also contains a supposed "invocation to the devil": *Palas aron ozinomas, Baske bano tudan donas,*

preliminary to general "magick" work—but it is used within the *Religion of Witchcraft*, which is to say *Wicca*, as a prelude to the invocation or "drawing down" of "Gods and Goddesses" (deities).

The first four lines (repeated three times):

> "Eko! Eko! Azarak!
> Eko! Eko! Zomelak!
> (Eko! Eko! Aradia![†]
> Eko! Eko! Kernunnos!)"

A possible continuation from original sources:[∞]

> "Zod-ru-koz e Zod-ru-koo,
> Zod-ru-goz e Goo-ru-moo!
> Eko! Eko! Hoo! Hoo! Hoo!"

Additional lines used from a French play:[*]

> "Bagahi laca bachahé,
> Lamac cahi achabahé, Karrelyos.
> Lamac, lamec bachalyos,
> Cabahagi sabalyos, Baryolas.
> Lagozatha cabyolas,
> Samahac et famyolas, Harrahya."

Geheamel cla orlay, Berec hé pantaras tay.

[†] Additions in parenthesis appear in the *Book of Shadows* only.

[∞] This portion does not appear in the original *Book of Shadows*.

[*] Used in the *Book of Shadows* and *Grimoire of Lady Sheba*.

And finally, the Gardnerian additions:‡

"Darksome night and shining moon,
East, then South, then West, then Noon;
Hearken to the Witches' Rune—
Here we come to call ye forth!

Earth and Water, Air and Fire,
Wand and Pentacle and Sword,
Work ye unto our desire,
Hearken ye unto our word!

Cords and Censer, Scourge and Knife,
Powers of the Witch's Blade—
Waken all ye into life,
Come ye as the Charm is made!

Queen of Heaven, Queen of Hell,
Horned Hunter of the Night—
Lend your Power to this Spell,
And Work our Will by Magic Rite!

By all the Power of Land and Sea,
By all the Might of Moon and Sun—
As we Will, so mote it be;
Chant the Spell and be it done!"

---

‡ Written by Gerald Gardner and Doreen Valiente;
when applied by the solitary *Witch*, the "*we*" and
"*us*" can be changed to "*I* " and "*me*" where
appropriate.

THE GODDESS & THE GOD
(AN APPRENTICE PRIMER)

The "Religion of Witchcraft and Magic" was referred to as *Wicca* by Gerald Gardner and thereafter has come to represent a standard for variegated modern revivals of "neopaganism"—spiritual pathways and personal lifestyles that are intended to reflect "ye olde tyme religion," "the old ways," ...the *pagan ways*.

Of course, the concept of "religion" does not mean the same thing to all people—and it is the treatment of the "magical lifestyle" and "grimoire practices" of *Witchcraft* as a "religion," which separates *Wicca* from other types of occult and metaphysical pursuits.

By definition, when we refer to "religion" we are evoking the idea of "Divinity," which is to say an individual's personal identification with, or personification of, "Deity." And by this we mean that which is representative of a "Supreme Being" or "Supreme Beingness" and even "Infinity." Since such is so incredibly "awesome" that it would be difficult to actually behold or appropriately represent directly, the various principles of "Cosmic Law," the observed cycles of action in Nature and Life, *&tc.* were all treated as the very "*deity archetypes*" personified in the ancient religions being revived today.

In contrast to many other popular religions of the common era—denominations of *Christianity*, factions of *Buddhism* and even *Islamic* practices—the revival of *Wicca-Witchcraft* has set itself apart from the rest with a reintroduction of the "Goddess." Heavy emphasis on "superiority" of the Goddess is really only strictly observed in certain traditions—"Dianic Covens" *&tc.*—where participation is reserved primarily to females practitioners. Otherwise, the deep contrast of a public religion involving a "Goddess" is really only so boldly distinguished in our mainstream perspective when compared to its blatant absence in the last several thousand years.

Ancient pagan traditions did not place any greater religious emphasis on one or another of the genders. The oldest pantheons—such as those in Mesopotamia from 6,000 years ago—did not even emphasize a "union of opposites" so much as they did an "absence of opposites," with each aspect or property of the Cosmos equally represented by, what we would define as, a "God" *and* "Goddess." This means that rather than observing solely a "Moon Goddess" in contrast to a "Solar God," ancient Babylonians (and Sumerians) perceived (and cataloged) "masculine" and "feminine" representations of *each* within the original "pagan" religions.

Duality and polarity are simply necessary factors or conditions for manifestation to occur—for action and movement to occur. The "division" of this is emphasized more strongly in modern *Wicca* than in other forms of neopaganism—lending to its reputation of being primarily a "Goddess Tradition" or "Goddess Worship." Although this is not as blatantly dominant in ancient pagan traditions as many in the New Age suggest, the emphasis seen today is most likely due to a corrective pendulum swing of extremism or revolt to an age of "patriarchal-dominant" presentations of "religion" and Divinity.

"*Traditional Witchcraft*"—which is essentially "*Celtic Witchcraft*" mixed with "*Italian Witchcraft*"—often focuses on the "Horned Goddess" and "Horned God," which is to say a "Crescent-crowned Lunar Goddess" and the "Antlered-headed God of the Wild." It is for this reason we see an emphasis on the Moon Goddess in the "Aradian Tradition" and why the Celtic-Druid deity Kernunnos (or Cernunnos) is so frequently invoked in *Wicca-Witchcraft* as the archetypal "Goddess and God of Witches."*

When it comes right down to it: aspects of *true* "religion" are seldom discussed in contemporary "New Age" literature or popular "*grimoires of witchcraft.*" In fact, although treated within the context of "neopaganism" or "religion"—with em-

---

* Another example lists "*Diana*" and "*Pan*" as predominant.

phasis on all various pantheons of deities drawn out of ancient mythologies—even the true and utmost highest considerations of "Divine" worship, as relayed in the deepest laden traditions of the most distant past, are often nonexistent in modern interpretations.

There are differences between actions taken for "religious prayer" versus "ritual spellcraft" and yet the goals and purposes are so similar: an individual is seeking to communicate an intention to something "greater than" this material existence, however that is perceived. A *Witch* believes that there is another realm overlapping, encompassing and yet intertwined with the Physical Universe; and "magical acts" are the mean of contacting or connecting with this "higher plane" and through it, having a greater effect on the events of the Physical Universe—tipping the scales of "quantum uncertainty" in their favor.

Most traditions will invoke specific archetypes or *Names* for those treated as one's own personal "patron deities." These are usually selected from a particular cultural paradigm or mythic pantheon that personally resonates with the practitioner. Alternatively, using rites as given (or derived) from the *Book of Shadows* employ a hybrid blend of Italian (*Strega*) and Celtic (*Druid*) lore for its "theology." Application of "religious dedication" to *magic* replaces any archaic ritual requirements, such as those found in grimoires, which may suggest threatening, exorcising or coercing dead spirits and demons to attain positive results.

When the Altar is appropriately oriented to the North, North-East or East: the *left side* is considered sacred to the *feminine*, the Moon, the Earth, the Waters and the Goddess; meanwhile the *right side* is treated as predominantly *masculine*, governing the Sky (or Airs), the Sun, Fire and the God. Within a *Witch's Circle*, Divine forces—dualistic qualities of the Goddess and God—are represented and acknowledged during rituals. This may be as simple as having a *Candle* present on the *Altar* to symbolize each. You may wish to even obtain or fashion an appropriate *Image* or *Statue* to go with it. The following general invocations[‡] may be made before the *Images* or *Signs* while lighting the *Candles*.

A Witch's Call to the Goddess

Goddess of the Starry Skies;
Goddess of the Fertile Plain;
Goddess of the Ocean Sighs;
Goddess of the Gentle Rain.
Hear my calling to you this hour.
Open wide the Gate of Mystic Light.
Awaken me with your graceful Power.

[‡] The present editor was unable to locate the source of these.

Aid me in my Magical Rite.

A Witch's Call to the God

Great God of the Forest Deep;
Master of the Animals and Sun.
Here in a world lost to sleep,
Now that the day is done [just begun].
I call to you in the Ancient Way,
Here in this Circle round.
I desire my Will to be displayed,
I call you to send your Powers down.

EXAMPLE: CASTING THE CIRCLE (GROUP LITURGY, VERSION 1998)†

The following ritual text is one example of "Casting the Circle" and this part of the rite does not include elements found in other parts of the *Handbook*; such as "Initiations into the Circle" or "Consecrations." As is common in a *Book of Shadows* or "secret grimoire," this script features only a dialogue formula, but not *what* to "visualize" or *how* to handle "energy" or any other ritual "actions"—as it is assumed that a *Witch* keeping written records of ceremonial verbiage, such as these, has

---

† Revised for Merlyn Stone's "*1998 Book of Shadows*" (the original version of *The Witch's Handbook*) used by the "Elven Fellowship Circle of Magick" (EFCOM) in Denver, Colorado.

been instructed in the basic magical applications elsewhere. Application of this "group liturgy" may be modified for solitary practitioners. [All four formulae are typically used.]

UNIVERSES FORMULA

Leader:	"As Above..."
Respondents:	"...So Below."
Leader:	"As Within..."
Respondents:	"...So Without."
Leader:	"As the Universe..."
Respondents:	"...So the Soul."

MAGIC CIRCLE FORMULA

East/Leader:	"We consecrate this Circle of Power to *Menw* and *Awen*."[∞]
South:	"May they hear our call and bless us with their grace."[√]
West:	"May the Elder Gods— the Ancient and Shin-

[∞] "*Menw*" and "*Awen*" are the Divine Names—or "God and Goddess" (respectively)—used in the original rites of the "Elven Fellowship Circle of Magick" (EFCOM).

[√] In *Sorcerer's Handbook*, this reads: "...bless us with power."

ning Ones—aid and
protect us."

North: "We stand at a threshold
between worlds veiled in
secrecy."*

WATCHTOWERS FORMULA

East: "ORO IBAH AOZPI—
Oh-roh; Ee-bah; Ah-oh-
zod-pee[25]—In the names
and letters of the Great
Eastern Quadrangle, I
invoke thee Spirits of
the Watchtower of the
East."[26]

South: "OIP TEAA PDOKE—
Oh-ee-peh; Teh-ah-ah;
Peh-doh-key—In the
names and letters of the

---

* In *Sorcerer's Handbook*, this reads: "...in a veil of
mystery."

25 The alternate version in the "*1998 Book of
Shadows*" adds the name "*Shem-ham-phor-ash*"
to the calls for each Watchtower.

26 This formula-type employs elements from the
"Watchtower Ceremony" (used by the Golden
Dawn, O.T.O., Aurum Solis and other magical
orders) based on a combination of the Chaldean
Tablets of Zoroaster and John Dee's Enochian
Magic.

	Great Southern Quadrangle, I invoke thee Spirits of the Watchtower of the South."
West:	"MPH ARSL GAIOL— Em-peh-heh; Arr-ess-el; Gah-ee-oh-leh—In the names and letters of the Great Western Quadrangle, I invoke thee Spirits of the Watchtower of the West."
North:	"MOR DIAL HKTG— Moh-arr; Dee-ah-leh; Heh-keh-teh-gah—In the names and letters of the Great Northern Quadrangle, I invoke thee Spirits of the Watchtower of the North."
East:	"May the presence of the Four Watchtowers be among us within this Magic Circle."

GUARDIANS/MASTERS FORMULA[27]

---

27 The alternate version in the "*1998 Book of Shadows*" includes an additional formula for

South:	"Then let us now conjure up and call forth the presence of the Four Masters to stand as Guardians at the Watchtowers and protect this Magic Circle."‡
West:	"And may their powers come with the wisdom to use it."
North:	"From the Northern City of *Falias*, I summon *Master Morfessa*. Bring the *Stone of Fal* and stand as Guardian of the North."
Respondents:	"Hail to the Guardian of the Watchtower of the North."†

---

calling the Dragon's Breath from the spirit of the four elemental dragons: "*Grail*" (Earth); "*Sarys*" (Air); "*Fafnyr*" (Fire) and "*Nalyon*" (Water).

‡   In *Sorcerer's Handbook*, this reads: "Let us now conjure the powers of the Masters."

†   This formula-type evokes names and attributes specific to the "Elven-Druid" or "Celtic-Faerie" traditions that regard the "Tuatha d'Anu" (Tuatha de Dannan); see *Elvenomicon* by Joshua Free, also available in the anthology: *Merlyn's Complete Book of Druidism: A Master Course in*

East:	"From the Eastern City of *Gorias*, I summon *Master Esras*. Bring the *Spear of Lugh* and stand as Guardian of the East."
Respondents:	"Hail to the Guardian of the Watchtower of the East."
South:	"From the Southern City of *Finias*, I summon *Master Uscias*. Bring the *Sword of Nuada* and stand as Guardian of the South."
Respondents:	"Hail to the Guardian of the Watchtower of the South."
West:	"From the Western City of *Murias*, I summon *Master Semias*. Bring the *Cauldron of Dagda* and stand as Guardian of the West."
Respondents:	"Hail to the Guardian of the Watchtower of the West."
North:	"May the powers of

Four Masters gather here
among us."

RITUAL FINALE & CLOSING RITES

If we are to fully treat the subject of a "Magic Circle" or *Witch's Circle* in the traditional sense, then there are a few more points-of-fact to advise in, before closing out this notebook. For starters, there is the matter of "Breaking the Circle" once it is cast, whether that is for emergencies during the ritual or even at the end of a rite. But, in order to discuss this properly, some semantic (vocabulary) clarification is required.

In this *Handbook*, "opening rites" or "starting procedures" are indicative of what we have consistently referred to as "Casting the Circle"—in the same sense as someone might "cast" some sticks or stones on the ground to divine an omen, or the way in which an artist "casts" the form of their creation. In some other literary sources, this same step may also be referred to as "Closing the Circle," which is to say "sealing" it shut as a "closed-system."

Separate from procedures used at the start of a ceremony, there will also be mention of "Opening the Circle." In this instance, we mean breaking the "hermetic seal" that separates the two conceptions of a "universe." In most spellbooks and grimoires, a *Witch* is instructed to *never* break the Circle—and the danger of this is imposed rather heavily in archaic work, such as the verbatim methodology of even the *Key of Solomon* and *Goetia*-type manuals that now seem wholly inappropriate to the Wise.

However, given that a Circle is "cast" as a mental image—or personal energetic creation that is set to "remain solid" for the duration of a ritual—it is highly appropriate that a *Witch* should knowingly "dissolve" or "extinguish" their creation until it is needed again. There are no concerns here over "lost" energy; and the individuals that would speak of such are not really *Aware* of the true properties of energy and its ability to be generated, at Will, by the *Self* as Spirit—the actual "I" or "I-AM" that is *using* a body to conduct the rituals.

If the Circle must be "opened" temporarily during a rite, it is customary to use a Ritual Blade (*Dagger* or *Athame*) and "cut" (acknowledge/postulate) an energetic "opening" (gateway) in the circle (traditionally in the East), which is then "resealed" before continuing the ceremony.

There is also the matter of the Code of Honor, seemingly long-forgotten in today's society, which is fully executed in traditional ceremonial and ritual magic. This means that if energies are summoned or presences are individually called to the Circle, then these should likewise be cordially thanked and dismissed—regardless of whatever *has* or *has not* taken place during the "working" portion of a ritual.[*] According to the original *Sorcerer's Handbook of Merlyn Stone*:—

> At the end of a rite, it is customary to work the preliminaries backwards: beginning with the thanking and dismissal of the God and Goddess (*Deities*); followed by the Elementals (*Guardians* and *Watchtowers*); and finally, the Extinguishing of the Circle. For the Elementals: go to the North and dismiss them at each direction in turn, working counter-clockwise to the West and so forth. Ask them to 'return to return promptly to their place of dwelling but to come to the Magic Circle when again called'.

> The final necessary part of the ritual is extinguishing and grounding any energies used to "Cast the Circle." This could be accomplished in multiple ways. Some practitioners move counter-clockwise around the

---

[*] The "working" portion of the ritual includes all work other from chapters/notebooks of *The Witch's Handbook*, conducted in between "Casting the Circle" and "Dissolving the Circle" as covered within the present chapter/notebook.

boundary *retracting* the band or ring of the Circle. Alternatively, a *Witch* could simply ground the energies with a single postulate —and if ritual actions are desired: stand in the center of the Circle with arms upraised, visualizing energies of the circle being sent down, deeper and deeper in to the ground, down to the fiery center of the Earth to be recycled and reformed.

EXAMPLE: DISSOLVING THE CIRCLE (GROUP LITURGY, VERSION 1998)†

MAGIC CIRCLE FORMULA

East/Leader:	"As we have come to this Magic Circle in love and friendship..."
South:	"...So do we leave the same way."
West:	"May we spread the peace and love that we have known here..."
North:	"...And radiate it out-wardly to the world."

---

† Revised for Merlyn Stone's "*1998 Book of Shadows*" (the original version of *The Witch's Handbook*) used by the "Elven Fellowship Circle of Magick" (EFCOM) in Denver, Colorado.

GUARDIANS/MASTERS FORMULA

East: "So now we ask the Ele mental Guardians called here to return to their duties in Nature."

South: "We thank you for atten- dance, watching over us and protecting this Magic Circle."

West: "Lords and Ladies of the Elves, Sylphs, and all Creatures of Faerie..."

North: "...Our thanks and bless- ing go with you for shar- ing this time with us."

WATCHTOWERS FORMULA

East: "Guardians of the Watchtowers of the East, Lords and Ladies of the Air Element, thank you for attending our rites. As you depart to your pleasant realms, we bid you a cordial hail and farewell."

Respondents: "Hail and farewell."

South: "Guardians of the

	Watchtowers of the South, Lords and Ladies of the Fire Element, thank you for attending our rites. As you depart to your pleasant realms, we bid you a cordial hail and farewell."
Respondents:	"Hail and farewell."
West:	"Guardians of the Watchtowers of the West, Lords and Ladies of the Water Element, thank you for attending our rites. As you depart to your pleasant realms, we bid you a cordial hail and farewell."
Respondents:	"Hail and farewell."
North:	"Guardians of the Watchtowers of the North, Lords and Ladies of the Earth Element, thank you for attending our rites. As you depart to your pleasant realms, we bid you a cordial hail and farewell."
Respondents:	"Hail and farewell."

UNIVERSES FORMULA

East:	"The magick work is done."
South:	"The mystic web has been woven of mortal mind, heart and soul."
West:	"Helpful to they who choose to follow the ways of the mighty spir its of our ancestors."
North:	"Baneful to those that choose to oppose the Elder Gods—the Ancient and Shinning Ones."

FINALE

Leader:	"The Circle is open but never broken. So Mote it be."
Respondents:	"So Mote it be."
Leader:	"The Rite is ended. Go in peace, love and unity. Blessed be."
Respondents:	"Blessed be All."

THE SABBATS & GROVE FESTIVALS

(Merlyn Stone, Spring-Summer '98)

A *Witch* will discover a wide diversity of flavors in the last hundred years of fundamental ritual texts concerning "Seasonal Festivals" or *Sabbats*— more so than any other aspect of *Witchcraft Tradition.* This is primarily due to a minimum of "ceremonial rites" or "*coven* specifics" in the Gardnerian *Book of Shadows*;[28] no mention at all in the *Book of Aradia* or other popularly excerpted "classical" *grimoires*; and since the *Sabbats* are religious elements of *Witchcraft*—rather than aspects of "practical magick"—only miniscule amounts of suggestion are put forth by esteemed "Magical Orders" (such as the Golden Dawn, *&tc.*) and even that usually only pertains to the "equinoxes."

It *is* true that there *are* ancient traditions and cultural folk-practices to support what is given in today's "New Age" presentations of "*Sabbats*" for

---

28 "The *Book of Shadows* is surprisingly inadequate in one aspect: the Eight Sabbats. For some reason, the rituals which the Book lays down for the Eight Sabbats are very sketchy indeed— nothing like as full and satisfying as the rest."— Janet and Stewart Farrar, *Eight Sabbats for Witches.*

Wicca and *neopaganism*—such as the "*Greater Sabbats*" (*Samhain, Imbolc, Beltane, Lughnassadh*)—which are drawn directly from Irish-Celtic customs and Druidic lore. This lends to the notion that practicing contemporary "*Wicca*" is essentially "*Celtic Witchcraft.*" The two "equinoxes" and two "solstices" constitute "*Lesser Sabbats*" each year. Revival observance of "equinoxes" in England began primarily with a reincorporation of modern Druidism by John Toland in 1717. But, we can be quite certain that the ancients were well aware of these cosmic events based on astronomical arrangement of their megalithic sites.

THE STANDARD WHEEL OF THE YEAR

There is a dual significance to pagan observations of the "Wheel of the Year"—a standardized "eightfold model" of the annual cycle—which are: *agricultural* and *astronomical*; elsewhere one might consider the division as *agricultural* (pertaining to *Land/Earth*) and *mytholographic (mythological)* or else *Solar*. Although a *Witch* may certainly examine the histories and folk traditions of their own preferred culture to find correlative customary rites for seasonal festivals, those that are observed in the "standard model" of modern *Neopaganism* are especially "Celtic"—if not "Druidic"—in origin.

Use of the word *"Sabbat"* seems to have originated in Western Europe during the 13th Century as a term to indicate a "seasonal meeting of *witches."* Modern *Wiccan* traditions continue to refer to their festival observations of the "Wheel of the Year" as *"Sabbats."* The word does not necessarily appear in *all* "New Age" or "neopagan" revivals—such as traditions oriented more heavily toward "Celtic" and "Druidic" overtones, which refer to the same days as "Grove Festivals"[29] or "Fire Festivals."[30] And of course, the term has an obvious relationship with the word *"Sabbath,"* meaning[‡] "a time of worship."[*]

When Gerald Gardner set down the original *Book of Shadows* (with assistance from Aleister Crowley and possibly Ross Nichols) as a foundation for modern *Wicca:* four traditional "Celtic Fire Festivals" were combined with the "solstices" and "equinoxes" to present *Eight Sabbats* for the "Wheel." Coupling these with observance of *thirt-*

---

29 The phrase "Grove Festival" appears in *Book of Pagan Rituals* by Herman Slater and in the works of Douglas Monroe.

30 The term "Fire Festival" was popularized in *The Golden Bough* by Sir James Frazer.

‡ Also from the Greek *sabatu*, meaning "to rest." As a result, "magick work" is not typically conducted on a Sabbat.

* This paragraph appears in *The Great Magickal Arcanum.*

een annual Full Moon "*Esbats*" provided this newer "standardized" 20th Century *Witchcraft religion* with "*21 Days of Power*" each year.

Ancient "Celtic" seasonal festivals—and similar ones observed throughout most indigenous cultures—marked key points in the year indicating *agricultural* significance (and similarly the breeding patterns of animals), which were relevant to farming communities. This was of particular importance to personal survival for these predominantly rural-country self-sufficient "pagan" lifestyles. With annual patterns in Nature on Earth being both easily observable and carrying practical significance, it would be easy to trace and incorporate historic "folk traditions" for each of the "*Greater Sabbats*"—*Samhain*, *Imbolc*, *Beltane* and *Lughnassadh*—with more numerous examples than space is allotted for in this notebook. Rather than observing growth cycles and animal behavior, monitoring "solstices" and "equinoxes" as "*sabbats*" requires potentially more detailed calculations, knowledge of astronomical data and even access to "Solar Temples" and/or observatories (ruins of which are found scattered all throughout Western Europe). This supports what many have suggested regarding *Witchcraft* and folk traditions: that observations of the "summer solstice" and "equinoxes" were likely imported from a Celestial-oriented "solar cult" (such as the Druids), rather than an "agricultural" one.

THE CELTIC FIRE FESTIVALS[†]

The Celtic year was not at first regulated by the solstices and equinoxes, but by some method connected with agriculture or with the seasons. Later, the year was a lunar one, and there is some evidence of attempts at synchronizing solar and lunar time. But time was mainly measured by the moon, while in all calculations night preceded day. Thus "*oidhche Samhain*" was the night preceding *Samhain* (November 1), not the following night.[∞] The usage survives in our "*sennight*" and "fortnight."

In early times the year had two, possibly three divisions, marking periods in pastoral or agricultural life, but it was afterward divided into four periods, while the year began with the winter division, opening at *Samhain*. A twofold, subdivided into a

---

[†] Selected excerpts from J.A. MacCulloch's *Religion of the Ancient Celts (1911)*; reprinted in the anthology "*Draconomicon-2: The Pheryllt Researches*" by Joshua Free. It is included here, as per the original notebooks, "to provide greater legitimacy to the 'pagan wheel' than is found in the *Book of Shadows* or the brands of ceremonial magic that inspired its practicality."

[∞] Many of these older traditions observe a "day's end" at sundown; meaning the period of a day is marked by one sundown until the following sundown—thus Samhain celebrations begin on the evening of October 31.

fourfold division is found in Irish texts, and may be tabulated as follows:

Geimredh (winter half)

1st Quarter, *Geimredh*, beginning with the festival of *Samhain*, November 1st.

2nd Quarter, *Earrach*, beginning February 1st. (Sometimes called *Oimelc*).

Samhradh (summer half)

3rd Quarter, *Samradh*, beginning with the festival of *Beltane*, May 1st. (Also called *Cet-samain*, 1st day of *Samonos*; Welsh *Cyntefyn*)

4th Quarter, *Foghamhar*, beginning with the festival of *Lughnassadh*, August 1st (Sometimes called *Brontroghain*).

None of the four fire festivals is connected with the times of equinox and solstice. This points to the fact that the original agricultural Celtic year was independent of these. But Midsummer day was also observed not only by the Celts, but by most European folk, the ritual resembling that of Beltane. The festivals of Beltane and Midsummer may have arisen independently, and entered into competition with each other. Or Beltane may have been an early pastoral festival marking the beginning of summer when the herds went out to pasture, and Midsummer a more purely agricultural or astronomical festival.

The Celtic festivals being primarily connected with agricultural and pastoral life, we find in their ritual survivals traces not only of a religious but of a magical view of things, of acts designed to assist the powers of life and growth.

THE EIGHT SABBATS FOR WITCHES[†]

NOVEMBER EVE (OCT 31 – NOV 1)

—Traditional Names: Samhain/Samhuinn [*sow'en*] ("Summer's End"), Festival of Ancestors and Spirits, Calen Gaeof, Samana/Samonios, Feast/Day of the Dead, Night of the Wild Hunt, All Saint's Day, All Soul's Day, All Hallows Eve/Halloween.

—Astrological: Sun is 15° of Scorpio.

—Summary/Symbols: Often treated as the "Pagan New Year"; a time to honor "dead names" (our ancestors); circles of skulls; dressing up in costumes; carving gourds/pumpkins into candlelit heads; bobbing for apples.

[†] Collected from the original Merlyn Stone notebooks. Additional suggestions for ceremonial application may be found in *The Druid's Handbook* and *Elvenomicon* by Joshua Free— both of which are contained in the anthology, *Merlyn's Complete Book of Druidism: A Master Course in Druidry for Modern Druids*.

—Elements: Earth, Northwest, Midnight, Winter.

—Celtic Deities: Gwyn ap Nudd, Samhan, Kerridwen, Morrigan.

—Essence & Incense: Apples, applewood, belladonna (nightshade), catnip, datura, hemp, mugwort, pomegranate, pumpkin/gourds, wormwood.

—Altar Candles: 2 black, 1 white.

—Sabbat Incantation: *"Dread Lord of the Shadows, God of Life and Giver of Life. Yet is the knowledge of thee, the knowledge of Death. Open wide, I pray thee, the Gates through which all must pass. Let our dear ones who have gone before, return this night to make merry with us. And when our time comes, as it must, O thou the Comforter, the Consoler, the Giver of Peace and Rest, we will enter thy realms gladly and unafraid; For we know that when rested and refreshed among our dear ones, we will be reborn again by thy grace, and the grace of the Great Mother. Let it be in the same place and the same time as our beloved ones. And may we meet and know and remember, and love them again. Descend, we pray thee, in thy servant and priest (name)."*[*]

WINTER SOLSTICE (DEC 21 – DEC 22)

—Traditional Names: Yule, Midwinter, Alban Arthuann ("Light of Arthur"), Jul, Saturnalia,

---

[*] Gerald Gardner, *Book of Shadows (1949).*

Finn's Day, Rebirth of the Sun King, Vigil Festival, Christmas.

—Astrological: Sun enters 0° of Capricorn.

—Summary/Symbols: Rebirth of the Sun God; the Yule-log; kissing under mistletoe, "holly and ivy"; decorating evergreen trees, bells, sunrise service.

—Elements: Earth, North, Midnight, Dark to Light.

—Celtic Deities: Kernunnos, Mabon.

—Essence & Incense: Bay/laurel, cedar, cinnamon, ginger, holly, ivy, juniper, mint, mistletoe, myrrh, nutmeg, pine, rosemary, sandalwood, valerian.

—Altar Candles: 1 green, 1 red, 1 white.

—Sabbat Incantation: " *Queen of the Moon, Queen of the Sun, Queen of the Heavens, Queen of the Stars, Queen of the Waters, Queen of the Earth, bring to us the Child of Promise! It is the Great Mother who giveth birth to Him; It is the Lord of Life who is born again; darkness and tears are set aside when the Sun shall come up early! Golden Sun of hill and mountain, illumine the land, illumine the world, illumine the seas, illumine the rivers, sorrows be laid down, joy to the world! Blessed be the Great Goddess, without beginning, without ending, everlasting to eternity. IO EVO HE!*[31] *Blessed be! IO EVO HE! Blessed be!*

31 Concerning the Calls: "Many of these have been

IO EVO HE! Blessed be!"*

FEBRURY EVE (JAN 31 – FEB 1)

—Traditional Names: Imbolc/Imbolg, Brighid's Day, Calen Geaef, Oimelc, Candlemas, Festival of Lights, Lupercalia, St. Blaise's Day, St. Valentine's Day, Snowdrop Festival, Groundhog's Day.

—Astrological: Sun is 15° of Aquarius.

—Summary/Symbols: Anticipation/conception of spring; hearth lighting; candle festival; corn-dolls.

—Elements: Air, Northeast, Dawn, Spring.

—Essence & Incense: Clover, dill, mace, rosemary, rowan, seaweed, snowdrop, white flower, willow.

—Celtic Deities: D'Anu, Brighid, Epona.

—Altar Candles: 2 white, 1 green.

—Sabbat Incantation: *"Dread Lord of Death and*

---

forgotten by us here; but we know they used cries of *IAU*, *HAU*, which seems much like the cry of the ancients: *EVO* or *EAVOE*. Much depends on the pronunciation if this be so. Other calls are: *IEHOUA* and *EHEIE*. Also: *HO HO HO ISE ISE ISE*. *'Tout tout, through and about'* and *'rentum tormentum'* are probably mispronounced attempts at a forgotten formula..."—*Gardnerian Book of Shadows*.

* Gerald Gardner and Doreen Valiente, *Book of Shadows (1957)*.

Resurrection, Of Life and the Giver of Life. (Lord within ourselves, whose name is Mystery of Mysteries, encourage our hearts, let thy Light crystallize itself in out blood),[32] fulfilling us with resurrection; For there is no part of us that is not of the Gods. Descend, we pray thee, upon thy servant and priest (name)."[*]

SPRING EQUINOX (MAR 21 – MAR 22)

—Traditional Names: Ostara, Akiti/Akitu (Mardukite Babylonian), Festival of Life, Alban Eiler, Vernal Equinox, Sheelah's Day, Bacchanalia, St. Patrick's Day, Easter/Eoster (Celtic festival of Ishtar-Inanna).

—Astrological: Sun enters 0° of Aries.

—Summary/Symbols: Rebirth of Earth Life; egg hunts and coloring; bird-watching; pastel colors.

—Elements: Air, East, Dawn, Light.

—Celtic Deities: Taliesen, Epona, Kerridwen.

—Essence & Incense: Broom, crocus, daffodil, fragrant flowers, Irish moss, jasmine, lavender, maple, narcissus, olive, woodruff.

—Altar Candles: 2 green, 1 white.

—Sabbat Incantation: *"We kindle fire this day. In the presence of the Holy Ones, without malice, without jealousy, without envy, without fear of*

---

32 From Aleister Crowley's "*Gnostic Mass.*"
*   Gerald Gardner, *Book of Shadows (1949).*

aught beneath the Sun but the High Gods. Thee we invoke, O Light of Life: be thou a bright flame before us; be thou a shining start above us; be thou a smooth path beneath us. Kindle thou within our hearts, a flame of love for our neighbors, to our foes, to our friends, to our kindred all, to all (Life) on this broad Earth. O merciful son of Kerridwen, from the lowliest thing that lives, to the Name which is highest of all."[*]

<u>MAY EVE (APR 30 – MAY 1)</u>

—Traditional Names: Beltane/Bhealltainn, Calen Mai ("First Light of May"), Festival of Flowers and Fire, Tana's Day, Walpurgisnacht (Walpurgis Night), Rudemas, May Day.

—Astrological: Sun is 15° of Taurus.

—Summary/Symbols: The Fires of Bel (bonfires); flower-gathering; Maypole (World Tree).

—Elements: Fire, Southeast, Noon, Summer.

—Celtic Deities: Bel/Belinos, Flora, Blodduwedd.

—Essence & Incense: Apple blossoms, birch, hawthorn, heather, honeysuckle, lilac, May blossoms, primrose, rosemary.

—Altar Candles: 2 white, 1 red.

—Sabbat Incantation: *"Oh, do not tell the (Priests) of our Art, for they would call it sin. But*

---

[*]   Gerald Gardner and Doreen Valiente, *Book of Shadows (1957)*.

*we shall be in the woods all night, a'conjuring
Summer in. And we bring you good news by word
of mouth, for women, cattle and corn: the Sun is
coming up from the South, by Oak and Ash and
Thorn. I invoke thee and call upon thee, O Mighty
Mother of us all, Bringer of all Fruitfulness. By
seed and root, by stem and bud, by leaf and flower
and fruit, by Life and Love, do we invoke thee, to
descend upon the body of thy servant and priestess
here."*[*]

SUMMER SOLSTICE (JUN 21 – JUN 22)

—Traditional Names: Litha, Alban Heruin or Alban Hefin, Feill-Sheathain, Midsummer, Festival of Oaks and Stones, St. John's Day.

—Astrological: Sun enters 0° of Cancer.

—Summary/Symbols: Height of the Sun, Needfires (bonfires), Faerie-calling, herb-gathering.

—Elements: Fire, South, Noon, Light to Dark.

—Celtic Deities: Arianrhod, Oghma/Ogmios, Huon.

—Essence & Incense: Copal, daisy, fern, frankincense, lavender, lemon, oak and mistletoe, red rose, saffron, St. John's Wort, sandalwood, vervain, yarrow.

—Altar Candles: 1 red, 1 white, 1 yellow.

---

[*]   Gerald Gardner, *Book of Shadows (1949)*, with
       borrowings from Rudyard Kipling's poetry.

—Sabbat Incantation: *"Great One of Heaven, Power of the Sun, we invoke thee in thine ancient names: Michael, Balin, Arthur, Lugh, Herne; come again, as of old, in this thy land. Lift up thy shining spear of light to protect us. Put to flight the powers of darkness. Give us fair woodlands and green fields, blossoming orchards and ripening corn. Bring us to stand upon thy hill of vision and show us the path to the lovely realms of the Gods. (The Spear to the Cauldron, the Lance to the Grail, Spirit to Flesh, Man to Woman, Sun to Earth.)$^\infty$ Dance ye about the Cauldron of Kerridwen the Goddess, and be ye blessed with the touch of this consecrated water; even as the Sun, the Lord of Life, arises in his strength in the sign of the Waters of Life."*[*]

AUGUST EVE (JUL 31 – AUG 1)

—Traditional Names: Lughnassadh/Lughnasa ("Marriage of Lugh"), Grain Festival, Festival of Bread, Calen Awst ("First Light of August"), First Harvest, Lammas.

—Astrological: Sun is 15° of Leo.

—Summary/Symbols: "Wedding Festival," grain harvest begins, "Lammas Towers" (bonfires competitions), spear-tossing (athletic competitions).

∞ "Incantation of the Great Rite for Midsummer."

[*] Gerald Gardner and Doreen Valiente, *Book of Shadows (1957)*.

—Elements: Water, Southwest, Sunset, Autumn.

—Celtic Deities: Lugh/Lug/Llew, D'Anu.

—Essence & Incense: Blackberries, corn/grain sheaf, furze, ginseng, heather, marigold, oats, rice, rye, straw, strawberry, sunflower.

—Altar Candles: 1 red, 1 yellow, 1 green.

—Sabbat Incantation:[†] *"O Mighty Mother of us all, Bringer of all Fruitfulness, give us fruits and grains, flocks and herds, and children to the tribe, that we may be mighty. By (the rose of thy love),[33] do thou descend upon the body of thy servant and priestess here."*[*]

AUTUMN EQUINOX (SEPT 21 – SEPT 22)

—Traditional Names: Mabon, Alban Elved, Harvest Equinox, Cornucopia, Festival of the Vine, Dionysus, Rosh Hashanah, Thanksgiving Day.

—Astrological: Sun enters 0° of Libra.

—Summary/Symbols: Produce harvest, the corn harvest, stalk-bundling, harvest feast, thanksgiving.

—Elements: Water, West, Dusk, Dark.

—Celtic Deities: Mabon, Bran, Branwen.

---

†   Also known as "Drawing Down the Moon for Lughnassadh."

33 "Thy rosy love" (Gardner); "rose of thy love" (Valiente).

*   Gerald Gardner, *Book of Shadows (1949)*.

—Essence & Incense: Acorns, Balm of Giliad, grape, hops, iris, mugwort, myrrh, pine-cone, sage, squash/melon, vines.

—Altar Candles: 1 red, 1 green, 1 black.[34]

—Sabbat Incantation: *"Farewell, O Sun, ever-returning Light, the Hidden God, who ever yet remains. He now departs to the Land of Youth through the Gates of Death to dwell enthroned, the judge of Gods and men, the horned leader of the hosts of air. Yet, as he stands unseen without the Circle, so dwelleth he within the sacred seed; the seed of new-reaped grain, the seed of flesh; Hidden in Earth, the marvelous seed of the stars. In him is Life, and Life is the Light of man, that which was never born and never dies. Therefore the (Wise Ones)[‡] weep not, but rejoice."[*]*

---

34 *The Druid's Handbook* lists "1 red, 1 white, 1 black."

‡ "Wise Ones" reads as "*Wicca*" in the original version.

* Gerald Gardner and Doreen Valiente, *Book of Shadows (1957)*.

THE ARTS OF SPELLCRAFT
(Merlyn Stone, Spring-Summer '98)

"Spells" are magically imbued intentions "cast" by a *Witch* to cause a change in the manner that energy manifests in the Physical Universe. Actual practice of the *Art* is far different than its portrayal in popular medias—but *real magic* can be very effective in tipping the scales of quantum uncertainty in the favor of the *Witch*. Operation of "spellcraft" is also referred to as "low magick," "sympathetic magic," or "ritual magic," depending on the source—and methods are far different than "prayer" or "meditation."

Purpose and function of the "Arts of Spellcraft" are precisely to apply dramatic representations, symbols and imagery in ritual to direct the personal energies of *desire* or *Will*. Though this says nothing regarding the nature of the inclinations and compulsions fueling such—and a *Witch* would be wise to execute the utmost care in treating any worldly matters, such as "wealth," "love," "fertility," &tc. But these things are freely given to that most cunning *Witch* that knows how to manifest them.

A *Witch* will practice the "Religion of *Witchcraft*" (*Wicca*) and likewise operate in service to one or another patron deities, often reviving various related cultural practices, and supplementing with some flavor of religious honor and regimen of *prayer.* This does not replace the function of "magick." Those who flocked to the *Craft* during the Middle Ages were Seekers of "Self-Help" and no longer satisfied with a dependency on religious institutions to serve as intermediaries for "divine intervention."

The *Witch* is not dependent on "Divine intervention," for we have been charged by the Creator Gods to carry all of the faculties necessary for success along our Pathway right within us. The teachings of the Ancients reveal that the individual is the only one that can be truly responsible for their life—and part of that responsibility includes an understanding of the orchestration of forces at work in this Game of Life, and just exactly what part you have to play in it. That is yours to decide. The Gods are notorious for "helping those who help themselves" and grow weary at the ceaseless wails raised up by the ignorant.

Traditionally "spellcraft" is defined simply as generating any transformation or manifestation to occur, in accordance with Will and Intention, in the Physical Universe. In the original *Sorcerer's Handbook*, it is taught that even the act of tying your shoes because you want them tied, is an example of Spellcraft. It doesn't matter what means are used: setting and meeting goals for change is a unique quality of the Human Condition that demonstrates reasoning on a higher level than what we are taught concerning the "nature of man as an animal." Yet, even animals have often demonstrated greater reason and sense than the average Human, when operating on automatic reactive mechanisms alone.

The idea that you can affect the future by acting in the present is an amazing point of Awareness that puts an individual at "Cause" in the universe and in the Game. This is no small realization, because it has allowed the Human Condition to elevate itself to the utmost on this planet—even if seldom tempered with the wisdom to properly carry out such a responsibility and stewardship of Earth. But the truth is: if your intention is to see something through, it doesn't really matter if you accomplish this by some form of esoteric telepathy or simply applying some old fashioned elbow grease, the result is the same (and this is even one of the tenets of "Freemasonry").

When practiced within the concentration of a Magic Circle, "spells" are energetically charged by focused and directed attentions of the *Witch*. Basic steps of consecrating "sacred space" (or the "Magic Circle") are employed; and such ritual forms of "spellcraft" include the magical and elemental objects and representations (discussed prior in *The Witch's Handbook*).

The working area can be as simple or elaborate as desired; but be certain that additional tools are included in the rite only if they actually help you to connect with the desired currents of energy and focus on the appropriate target.

Virtually every tradition in the "New Age" demonstrates ritualism differently, and this also applies to teaching the "Arts of Spellcraft." Starting in the 1980's, it seems to have become a growing trend to publish a personal "spellbook," "Book of Shadows" or "magical recipe book." A modern *Witch* will find no shortage of supplemental and complimentary materials on the market in this regard. However, by following the general guidelines of "magic" and "ritual" and developing a comfortable familiarity with the practice of ceremonious rites within the *Witchcraft* tradition, a *Witch* can also just as effectively develop their own "spells."

It is actually far more empowering to develop your own "rituals" and "spells." One of the reasons is that many "spellbooks" will suggest the incorporation of specific "tools," "herbs," "objects" and "words" that may be quite effective for the individual that wrote them down and presumably understood the significance behind the selection of each, but this may not be the case for a newcomer that happens upon the book. Such individuals tend to follow to closely to "instruction" and apply very little of their own "intention" to the operations—

and the results speak for themselves.

We are fast approaching the 21st Century and there is an entire esoteric library of background information and applicable lore now available to any *Witch* that seeks a greater understanding of the "hows" and "whys" of the occult and practical mysticism. But, even without such rigorous studies, the practice of "magick" has been demonstrated effective when instructed properly—as was discovered to be the case with our former version of *The Sorcerer's Handbook*. In this present edition, we have simply placed an even greater emphasis and focus on the legacy of *Wicca* and the *Witchcraft* tradition than the earlier publication.

Basic skills and ritual techniques of the former *Sorcerer's Handbook* all still apply to practice of "spellcraft" within the *Witchcraft* tradition. Quite simply: "magick is magick." Whatever works in one application does so because it follows the basic principles governing all workable magic, regardless of what flavor or patina it may be given.

It was quite customary for *Witches* and *Wizards* to keep "Magical Diaries" and notebooks to record the details of their "rites" in order to figure out these "governing workable principles" for themselves. Too often a modern practitioner will simply surround themselves with piles of notebooks and grimoires from *others* without ever actually holding any *personal* reality on the nature of the true magic alluded to—such as can only be worked out and experienced by an individual for and as *Self.*

THE SEVENFOLD SPELLCRAFT FORMULA

Basic prerequisites for "spellcraft" include a practiced ability to be grounded, focused, use breathing techniques, operate rituals within a Magic Circle, apply visualization and handle energy. [In some *covens* and training groups, the application of "spellcraft" is not introduced to an *Initiate* until after a proper mastery of these former techniques is demonstrated.]

Ritual "spells" tend to also include objects and graphic representations of the intention (and/or target)—pictures, symbols, statuary, candles, herbs, stones, talismans, personal items, hair, nail-clippings, &tc.

All other considerations being made, the "Sevenfold Spellcraft Formula"* is given as follows:

1. Casting a Circle (conjuring the "Magic Circle")
2. Calling the Corners (Elementals, Guardians,

---

* Developed for the "*1998 Book of Shadows*" used by the "Elven Fellowship Circle of Magick."

&tc.)
3. Raising Energy (personal mixed with summoned)
4. Visualization (seeing the change as taken place)
5. Releasing Energy (send toward the "target")
6. Dismissal of Spirits (closing rites and formalities)
7. Extinguishing the Circle (neutralizing residual)

MAGIC AND THE MOON

A *"lunar cycle"* is an observed period of time that it requires for the Moon to complete an orbit around the Earth. In fact, the word "month" would seem to be semantically connected to "moon" and its cycles. These cycles can be measured as both "sidereal" or "synodic" periods. A *sidereal* month is approximately 27.3 days—marking the time it takes the Moon to physically complete an orbit. A *synodic* month also takes into consideration the rotation/spin and orbit motions of the Earth, which is measured out to be approximately 29.5 days. The average between these two is what the *Witch* observes as a *"Lunar Month"* of 28 days.

There are lunar-oriented calendars dating back to the ancient Sumerians and Babylonias, which consist of 29 and 30-day months. Although common

Witchcraft "spellbooks" emphasize the *"Full Moon"* as an energetic apex of the monthly cycle, other various "magical lore" exists ascribing properties or correspondences also to the *"New Moon,"* *"waning phase," "waxing phase,"* the *"Gibbous"* (or three-quarter moon), the *"Quarter"* (or half-visible moon) and the *"Crescent."*

A *"New Moon"* is the energetic "low-tide" threshold of the monthly or lunar cycle, when the Moon is perceived to be invisible or darkened, at least from the perspective of the Earth planet. The *"New Moon"* is a peak point that ends the *"waning"* phase. The *ol' wives' tales* of Europe reveal that a *"New Moon"* is the time of month when a *Witch's* power is "weakest" (as opposed to the *"Full Moon"*), because it has spent two weeks *"waning."* After a *"New Moon,"* the *Witch's* power *"waxes"* ("grows") until the next *"Full Moon."*

Aside from properties attributed to "Dark Power" (which may be associated with the *"New Moon"*), there are relatively very few "magickal practices" (other than meditation, divination and passive exercises) performed within the original *Wiccan* tradition at the *"New Moon"*—although there are some *covens* that do observe a secondary *"Esbat"*‡ observance on this eve and others that practice "banishing rites" (when one wishes to rid themsel-

---

‡ "Secondary" to the *"Full Moon"* as the primary monthly *Esbat*.

ves of something).

And as the name suggests, the "*New Moon*" begins the month or lunar cycle—written as "day zero" on most lunar calendars. This means when a "spellbook" or "grimoire" recommends a rite be performed, for example, on the "sixth night of the moon," it refers to the sixth night after the "*New Moon.*"

For "magical timing" purposes, *Witches* and *Wizards* have assigned additional titles for two other significant "*New Moons*" for their work. The "*sidhe moon*"† or "*faerie moon*" is named after the "elemental folk" that are acknowledged as more active during dark moons—whereas the Human Condition seems to find greater energetic charge during bright moons. In other *Wiccan* lore, these "*Dark Moons*" or "*Black Moons*" refer to the second time the "*New Moon*" phenomenon occurs in a single calender month.* It is treated as having all the properties and significance of a "*New Moon*" multiplied one-hundred times.

At the height of the "*waxing*" phase, the Moon is completely visible from the Earth as is considered "*Full.*" Traditionally, the "*Full Moon*" is the time

---

†   "Sidhe" pronounced "*shee,*" referring to the Celtic Faerie Folk.

*   Given that there are thirteen lunar cycles in a solar year, this is typical to occur once annually.

of the month when a *Witch's* power soars. In fact, grimoires and spellbooks suggest most of their ritual performances for this eve—particularly if the "rite" is intended to *invoke* or draw something *toward* (such as in "attractive" magic for "wealth" and "love," &tc).

For purposes of "magical timing," *Witches* and *Wizards* have classified two other types of "*Full Moon*" in their lore. For example, a "*Blood Moon*" occurs when the Moon visibly appears "blood red." This typically occurs during the autumn season, or under the proper conditions of a "lunar eclipse" (which only take place during a "*Full Moon*"). The second type is called a "*Blue Moon*," which unlike the former, is not named for its color. The "*Blue Moon*" is the second occurrence of the "*Full Moon*" phenomenon within a single "solar month," magnifying the significance of the "*Full Moon*" one-hundred fold.

When examining modern "moon lore," the lunar calendar used in the Western World is also referred to as the "Farmer's Moons"—hinting at the original agricultural significance of these observations. Each of the "*Full Moons*" are named, beginning with the full moon of December or that falls closest to the Winter Solstice.

December (Winter Solstice): "Oak Moon"

January: "Wolf Moon"

February (Imbolc): "Storm Moon"

March (Spring Equinox): "Hare Moon"

April: "Seed Moon"

May (Beltane): "Dryad Moon"

June (Summer Solstice): "Mead Moon"

July: "Herb Moon"

August (Lughnassadh): "Barley Moon"

September (Autumn Equinox): "Harvest Moon"

October (Samhain): "Hunter's Moon"

November: "Snow Moon"

DRAWING DOWN THE MOON
(& THE FIVEFOLD KISS)

Aradian and *Gardnerian* traditions place supreme emphasis on the "High Priestess" as leader of a *coven.* In many respects, this custom is traced back to ancient pagan temples, when a "High Priestess" would *invoke* the "Goddess" and allow her own body to become a living vessel of the "Divine." In modern *Wicca*, this is referred to as "Drawing Down The Moon."‡ The practice is commonly

---

‡   These practices are given in the original 1949 edition of *Book of Shadows* developed by Gerald Gardner with Aleister Crowley.

linked with another *coven* tradition known as the "Fivefold Kiss" or "Fivefold Blessing."

According to original drafts of the *Book of Shadows*, the High Priestess assumes the "Goddess Position" (arms crossed) while standing in front of the altar.[35] The High Priest,[∞] kneeling in front of her, then draws a "pentacle" on her body with the "phallus-headed wand" and speaks:

> "I invoke and beseech Thee, O Mighty Mother of all Life and Fertility. By Seed and Root; by Stem and Bud; by Leaf and Flower and Fruit; by Life and Love, do I invoke Thee to descend into the body of thy servant and High Priestess [name]."

The "Fivefold Kiss" or "Fivefold Blessing" is then applied. Each member of the *coven*, in turn, comes

---

35 The High Priestess speaks (*from the north*): "As we breathe deeply in and out, it is not just air we take in; it is the soft silver light of the Moon, symbol of our Lady. With every pore of our bodies, we breathe in an out. And so does this Circle become a fitting place four our Lady's presence." (*raising arms*) "We are the Children of the Moon. We are born of shining light. When the Moon shoots forth a ray, we see within it the Goddess and ourselves."—*Outer Court Book of Shadows* (Ed Fitch).

∞ Referred to as a "Magus" in the original *Book of Shadows*.

before the High Priestess (now consecrated as a representative of the "Moon Goddess") and applies the following actions and incantations:

Kissing the feet: "Blessed be thy feet, that have carried thee in these ways."

Kissing the knees: "Blessed be thy knees, that shall kneel at the sacred altar."

Kissing the womb: "Blessed be thy womb, without which we would not be."

Kissing the breasts: "Blessed be thy breasts, formed in beauty and strength."

Kissing the lips: "Blessed be thy lips, which shall speak the sacred names."

ASTROLOGY AND THE MOON

Much as the Sun appears to be "backed" by the Celestial Sphere of "Zodiac Constellations" during the course of a year, so too does the Moon appear to travel through the "Twelve Houses" of astrology (from the perspective of Earth) in the period of a single month. This also means that the Moon only occupies each "sign" of the zodiac for a little more than two days.

The practice of treating a "lunar zodiac" with significance may be traced back to Astral Wizards of ancient Babylon—those that marked down the shifting of the starry skies with great precision. Thereafter, the Persian Magi, Arabs and the Orient all borrowed from this lore—each one applying their own mystical attributes and omens for consideration. For purposes of *Witchcraft* and keeping with its tradition of "following the moon," the significances of the "lunar zodiac" may be tracked and even incorporated into "practical magic" and "spellcraft."

Moon in Aries—optimism, outgoingness, opinions, impulsiveness, new beginnings, alchemy and fire magick.

Moon in Taurus—artistic, determined, overcautious, steadfast, habitat, solidity, physical/senses, new beginnings (with longevity in mind).

Moon in Gemini—versatility, wit, superficiality, manipulation, fluctuation/inconsistency, shortcuts, recreation, new beginnings (requiring external assistance).

Moon in Cancer—sympathy, protection, possessiveness, emotional, growth, family, relationships.

Moon in Leo—creativity, fun-loving, self-indulgent, overbearing, emotional healing, attraction, outer presentations, Hermetic magick.

Moon in Virgo—meticulousness, responsibility, stress, orthodox/standard, conformity, detailing, leadership, structure/hierarchies, schedules (cycles).

Moon in Libra—creativity, diplomacy, indecisiveness, frivolousness, introspection, meditation, enchantment, glamour.

Moon in Scorpio—ambition, emotion, secretiveness, dominance, increased awareness, karmic agreements, psychic/psionic, interconnectivity (entanglement).

Moon in Sagittarius—adventurous, open-mindedness, restlessness, irresponsibility, confidence, expansion, imagination, travel and growth.

Moon in Capricorn—responsibility, patience, materialistic, pessimism, foundations, regulations, structure (physical), tradition.

Moon in Aquarius—idealism, tolerance, tactlessness, fixedness, healing (physical), breaking habits, purification, personal transformation.

Moon in Pisces—sensitivity, vagueness, discontent, secrets/hidden, dreams, intuition, prayer, meditation, spiritual development.

MAGIC AND THE PLANETS

Ancient astronomical observers were also mystics and philosophers; they were the mathematicians and scientists of an age long past. These, soon to be known as, astrologers successfully followed the motions of the "visible planets" of the ancient world, which by their consideration, included the Moon and Sun. The others being: Mercury, Venus, Mars, Jupiter and Saturn—which are all apparent in the night sky, even without benefit of additional technological advancements and telescopes.

Each of the seven ancient planets correlates to not only seven notes of audible music and seven shades of a visible spectrum, but also the seven divisions observed between Earth and Infinity at ancient temples in Mesopotamia—and particularly Babylon—where the seven planets signified "Gates" that one would pass on the "Ladder of Ascension" (or "Ladder of Lights") as the Spirit makes its journey back to Source. Of course, this is not a guaranteed direction of travel; Ascension is not a reality for those that do not rise up above the trivialities of mundane existence and its gravity.

For the purpose of spellcraft, *Witches* observe that each day of the week is ruled by a planet—and when considering what some call "planetary hours," the first hour of daylight corresponds strongly to that ruling planet's influence. Many grimoires of ceremonial magic classify their pantheons or hierarchies of spirits based on their governing planets. These correlations are used by magical practitioners to determine the "most favorable time" to make contact with a particular spirit or current of energy. *Witches* commonly incorporate these correspondences to their "spellcraft."

Sunday (the Sun)—leadership, sacredness, solar observations, success magick, fire element.

Monday (the Moon)—faerie magick, psychic/psionic development, water element.

Tuesday (Mars)—courage, protection magick, military endeavors, victory/overcoming.

Wednesday (Mercury)—communication, divination, intellect, mental development, air element.

Thursday (Jupiter)—animals, business ventures, celebration, expansion, wealth acquisition.

Friday (Venus)—arts, beauty, enchantments, fertility, friendship, growth, love, earth element.

Saturday (Saturn)—banishing, binding,
cursing, hidden influences, initiation,
secrets.

THE COLOR OF MAGIC

Color plays a significant role in nearly all aspects
of the Human experience, to which, mysticism and
metaphysics are no exception. Everything from the
ritual garments (robes, cloaks, &tc.) to the altar
dressings; from the candle selection to the decora-
tion of elemental tools—all objects employed in
spellcraft and ritual magic (or even encountered in
everyday life) carry a certain "tone" or "quality"
that registers from their color. This becomes particularly important when a *Witch* is focusing their
attentions on the magical work.

When the Forces of Nature are encountered in a
Witch's energy practices, the various frequencies
are likened to the spectrum of visible of light—
likewise relayed as "Rays of Light." One sees this
aspect come into play with various lore—such as
the "*chakras*" and "*auras*"—which is often incorporated into modern *Witchcraft* traditions. But to
be semantically clear and scientifically accurate: it
is virtually impossible to consider facets of *color*
symbolism without dealing with the subject of
Light—for Light is the very medium that allows us
to perceive the existence of color.

It is not difficult to demonstrate the simple truth that colors carry different energetic qualities, and in the "magical traditions," they are given a certain universal significance based on the way they can make us "feel"—or more preferably, how they assist us to focus on a specific type of energy. The most basic demonstration of this appears in the colors selected for "elemental candles" that a *Witch* sets out to distinguish the "Quarters." These facets of perception and understanding all combine to provide the magical experience for a *Witch* during ritualized spellcraft and other operations of magic.

> White—akasha, blessings, consciousness, the entire visual electromagnetic spectrum, the full moon, the higher self, ice and snow, protection, purity, spiritual strength, truth and white magic.

> Red—blood, chaos, courage, fire element, love magic, mars, passion, personal strength, red magic, reproductive energies, sexuality, vigor.

> Orange (red+yellow)—attraction, business matters, charisma, courage, joy, legal matters, orange magic, personal magnetism, pleasure, pride, self-confidence, success, the sun.

> Yellow—academics, air element, alertness,

awareness, communication, confidence, logic, the mind, optimism, philosophy, spiritual development, the sun, yellow magic.

Green (yellow+blue)—balance, beauty, compassion, earth element, ecological (animals, plants, trees), envy, fertility magic, fortune, green magic, growth magic, healing magic, jealousy, physical appearance (glamour), renewal, venus.

Blue—awareness, blue magic, creativity, emotions, enchantment, glamour, illusion, imagination, jupiter, loneliness, peace, spiritual healing, spiritual protection, tranquility, water element.

Indigo (blue+red)—mercury, personal magnetism, psychic ability, reversal magic, spirits, storm magic, third eye (brow chakra), weather influence.

Violet (red+blue)—astral work, connectedness, healing magic, personal power, saturn, spiritual power, royalty, willpower and wisdom.

Brown—animals (protection and healing), business (prosperity), discrimination, earth element, energy clots (in auras), the home (protection), temperance, wealth magic, woodland spirits.

Gray—the astral, awakening, cancellation (magic), initiation, intuition, neutrality, the Otherworld, stalemate, threshold portals (dimensions/planes).

Silver—the astral, awareness, clarity, clearing, creativity, faerie folk, femininity, fertility magic (pregnancy), journeys, lunar cycles, mirrors, the moon, the Otherworld, wisdom.

Pink (red+white)—chastity, compassion, clearing, love magic, meditation, moderation, modesty, morality, purity, true love, truthfulness, virtue.

Black—black magic, clearing (purification), curses, death, hidden influences, invisibility (magic), loss, necromancy (spirits), resentment, the unknown.

CANDLE MAGIC & SPELLCRAFT*

"Beeswax" candles have a long-standing tradition of use in *Witchcraft*. Their application to rituals and spellcraft is based on color—which correlates to the representative energy that a *Witch* is to focus on during the magical working. Prior to and during

---

* Appearing here verbatim from the "*Sorcerer's Handbook.*"

the operation—as with all tools of magic—the candles are *charged* with an intention or to be a sympathetic representation of a particular object or "target."

Candles—or some representation of Light—are employed in virtually all magical operations; but as a standalone nonspecific system, "candle magick" is also an effective form of spellcraft, placing particular emphasis on use of candles as an energetic catalyst and focal tool. Of course, incense, herbs and other tools may also be employed. Whatever each candle represents may be vocalized during the working. No other specific "jargon" or "incantation" need be memorized to cast spells: "candle magick" requires imagination and creativity to be effective.

Just as a *Witch* is best able to focus and concentrate their energies best by creating a microcosm of the universe when creating sacred space—or casting a circle—so too does "candle magick" operate best when performed at an altar. This all represents a "chessboard" for the Game of Reality to play out on. By manipulating the symbols on a representative playing field, the desired change is manifested first in consciousness and then projected outward like a beacon into the world-at-large.

If drawing something *to* you, use a candle to represent yourself and one (or more) for energies you want to attract. In the practice of spellcraft, candles are "symbols" representing "solids." For several successive nights—usually three or seven —the *Witch* is to perform the working, each time moving the candle (that represents the external energy) closer to yours. The opposite motion is employed for reversals and banishing spells.

The candle representing *you* should always be placed in the center of the working area or altar— since the *Witch* plays this Game out from the centralized perspective of *Self.* It remains fixed and unmoved in the center always—the other candles and energies are arranged and move around *it*. Words and names may also be written on the candles (and some *Witches* believe it is more powerful to do this in Runes, Ogham characters or some other obscure alphabet). Intentions and affirmations are made whenever lighting a candle and also before one is moved (if applicable).

The following are basic examples demonstrating application of "candle magick" for spellcraft. A *Witch* is encouraged to develop their own ritual texts—with incantations or affirmations—as needed.

> AFFAIRS—to break up a love affair: use two candles to represent the people involved; a black candle for the breakup; a brown for the dying love; and a light green

to incite jealousy and discord.

BAD HABITS—to overcome a bad habit: place a black candle in the middle representing the habit itself; surround it with white candles symbolizing defeat of it.

DREAMS—to invoke prophetic dreams: surround your candle with a blue candle for peace and tranquility (required for restful sleep); use an orange to represent what you want to dream about; and a white for truth and sincerity of vision.

FEAR—to overcome emotions of fear: surround your candle with several orange candles representing personal strength and self-confidence; and a white for purity of thought.

JEALOUSY—to arouse jealousy in another: surround their candle with a few brown candles for hesitation and uncertainty; use light green candles to represent discord, illness, and of course, jealousy.

MEDITATION—to aid any acts of prayer or meditation: surround your candle with light blue candles for peace and tranquility.

POWER—to increase persuasion over people: take both your candle and the candle representing the subject and place them on the altar. Each day, move their candle closer to yours, symbolizing the magnetism. Also, surround your candle with purple for power and an orange candle demonstrating the attractive pull itself.

SPELLJAMMING—to remove a spell, hex or curse: surround your candle with red for strength and vigor; and white for purity and sincerity. Put a black and brown candle on either side. Black symbolizes the cursed spell and brown represents the uncertainty of its caster. Move the black candle towards the brown (and away from yours) each day of the working to deflect their spell.

HERBCRAFT—BY LEAF, STEM & BUD*

The practice of "herbalism" or "herbcraft" is an inherent part of both the ritual magic and folk customs found in *Witchcraft*. Use of flowers, leaves, plants, roots and tree-parts, as found in Nature (or reared in a personal garden) appears throughout ceremonial texts and rites of spellcraft—all based on a combination of physical traits and metaphysical properties or correspondences. This secret knowledge of Nature is studied by *Witches* and *Wizards*, preserving the lore once known exclusively to the Priests and Priestesses and eventually

---

* Section reprinted in "*The Great Magickal Arcanum.*"

the *Gypsy-Witch* and rural-pagan apothecaries through the Middle Ages.

Today, pharmaceutical companies profit from synthesizing the same lore. All common medicines now used are synthesized compounds based on the properties of the same natural herbs and plants that have been in use for thousands of years. As opposed to commercializing the planet, *Witches* are known for executing greater "care" in their treatment of Nature when removing any parts of it; being careful to "use" but not "abuse" Nature—because obviously all herbal work requires harvesting or removing part of a plant or tree.

Respect and reverence is observed whenever a *Witch* takes anything from Nature. A knife used strictly for cutting herbs should be ritually consecrated for that purpose. Traditionally, a small white-handled (or bone-handled) *Dagger-knife* or *Sickle* is used—and sometimes called a *Boline.* Many *Witches* prefer to tend to (and harvest) herbs from their own gardens—and so it is not uncommon for a *Witch* to maintain a personal herb garden (or "*Witch's Garden*"); in fact, this is just one popular aspect of the type of "natural sustainable-living" observed even today among many pagans, rural or otherwise.

When necessary, most metaphysical and "New Age" retail outlets stock a supply of various herbs that are useful for "magical operations" and spell-craft. For any therapeutic or medicinal purposes, a *Witch* would want to acquire a fresher supply, such as may be stocked by herb-specific natural-type groceries and health stores. When treating living plants, care should be taken not to needlessly tear or damage the plant, particularly if only a part of it is removed and it is left to continue growing. The blade cut should be a single sure upward motion, removed silently, after first asking *permission* and uttering the statement (with intention): "*With this strike, may you grow stronger*"—and a "*Thank you*" afterward.

It should be noted here that practices and lore of "magical herbalism" differs from the type of "al-chemical-apothecary" knowledge that is used to treat ailments. There is an obvious difference between the presence of an herb scattered about the altar, or rubbed on a candle, or sewn up in a square of colored fabric, or cast into a metal pot filled with alcohol to burn, or even as incense—versus the preparation of tinctures and extracts intended for personal consumption. For our present purposes within the scope of this book, we are most concerned with "magical herbalism."

The above being stated: a *Witch* could also boil potent tinctures or steep herbs in water (as a tea); or bottle herbs in alcohol;‡ etc. etc. Most natural food

---

‡ Never boil alcohol.

outlets actually sell enhanced extracts in dropper bottles (typically in the vitamin section). These are excellent for experimenting in personal health and self-treatment because of their levels of potency. Yet sometimes, extreme potency is the opposite of what is sought.

In homeopathic practices, extracts are then reduced to a point where the molecular structure of the herb used is all but dissolved, leaving on a trace resonance. A practitioner will want to seek out additional information from multiple sources before proceeding in this area.

Within the *Witchcraft* tradition, practices of "magical herbalism" appear most often when applying *Incense*—or even anointing *Oils* and personal *Perfumes*—to rites and spellcraft. Additionally, various folklore concerning "charms" suggests a long-standing tradition of carrying various flowers, leaves and herb-filled sachet-pouches as *Amulets* to ward away particular types of misfortune and illness. For example, in the 1960's, the "lucky" four-leafed *Clover* (or the larger Irish *Shamrock*) was frequently carried by those wishing to "ward away" military service (or in this case, avoid the "draft").

Lunar Work (the Moon)—frankincense, sandalwood.

Love and Romance—cinnamon, rose,

patchouli, sandalwood.

Peace and Serenity—bay (laurel), sandal-wood.

Wealth and Business—cedar, cloves, nut-meg, poppy seed.

Studying—cinnamon, rosemary.

Success and Charisma—benzoin, cinna-mon, dragon's blood.

Protection—frankincense, rosemary, san-dalwood.

Examining a few other examples: *Nettles* is carried to protect against evil and overcome fear; a wreath of *Mistletoe* is present to ease pain during child-birth; *Vervain* is carried to escape one's enemies; *Acorns* are worn to remain youthful and vigorous; fishermen carried *Hawthorn* sprigs to ensure their success at sea; the list goes on and on... A close ex-amination will reveal that each tradition—and even each regional culture—maintains some type of lore concerning use of local vegetation.

All-Spice—prosperity, relaxation.

Apple—love, happiness, relaxation.

Camphor—psychic power, clearing.

Cinnamon—protection, sexual vigor.

Eucalyptus—healing, purification.

Jasmine—love, sleep, relaxation.

Musk—courage, sexual prowess.

Myrrh—protection, purification, spelljamming.

Patchouli—peace of mind, sexual confidence.

Rose—love, peace, harmony, unity.

Sandalwood—healing, protection.

Some popular incense mixtures are known as "temple blends"—lore of which is retained in the classical grimoires of "*Medieval magic.*" For example: the "*Sacred Book of Magic of Abramelin the Mage*" is composed of *Cedar* (or *Aloe*) balm mixed with *gum* and *storax*. The "*Key of Solomon*" suggests blending many sweet smelling *gums*, *Aloe*, *Nutmeg* and *Musk*. Another common multipurpose "temple blend" is made from equal parts *Frankincense*, *Myrrh* and *Sandalwood*—in fact, these essences appear quite frequently in operations of "ceremonial magic."

A *Witch* can also make their own small "blocks" or "cones" of *Incense* from a dough—even a thin stick could have dough worked around it. The charcoal-free recipe formula call for (6 parts) powdered cedar, pine or sandalwood; (2 parts) powdered frankincense, myrrh or benzoin; (1 part) ground orris root; (6 drops) of fragrant oil; and (4 parts) some other powdered incense blend. This is all mixed together with tragacanth gum-glue and worked like a baker's dough.[36]

Amulet-Bags—or *"Sachets"*—are made from pouches; or the *Witch* may fashion an appropriate bag using a four-inch square swatch of cloth (of an appropriate color); herbs and small items are placed in the center of the square and then the corners are brought together and tied up as a pouch. Alternatively, you could weave a draw-string around the outside of a cloth circle, add the items, and then pull it closed and cinch it up.

According to popular lore: three, seven or nine herbs (or items) are added to a single *Amulet-Bag* before it is *consecrated* and *charged* with a ritual-ized spell. [To achieve the desired effect, it may then be carried, slept on (under the pillow) or giv-en away; whichever seems most appropriate.]

> PROTECTION (white)—ash, basil, bay, dill, fennel, mistletoe, mugwort, periwinkle, rosemary, rowan, saint john's wort, trefoil, vervain.

---

36 Scott Cunningham recommends the addition of *Saltpeter* (*potassium nitrate*) to the proportion of 10% of the total mixture (prior to the incorporation of the gum glue), which acts as a burn accelerator and keeps the finished product from repeatedly extinguishing once ignited.

HEALING (blue)—cinnamon, eucalyptus, garlic, lavender, myrrh, rosemary, saffron, sage, sandalwood.

LOVE (red)—apple, coriander, dragon's blood, jasmine, lavender, mandrake, marjoram, rose, rosemary, vervain, yarrow.

WEALTH/PROSPERITY (green)—basil, benzoin, cinnamon, clove, dill, nutmeg, patchouli, sage.

RITES OF INITIATION
(Merlyn Stone, Spring '98)

Matters of *Initiation* widely separate various *Wiccan* traditions representing the modern *Witchcraft* movement. Significance behind *Initiation* is skewered in many portrayals—often reduced to exercises of egotism and/or control. Certain tenets set down in Gerald Gardner's original *Book of Shadows (*and other traditional beliefs concerning "How a *Witch* should operate") often restricted access to the *Wiccan* legacy exclusively to "*Covens*" and "*Groves*" throughout its development during the 20th Century. Of course, today, things are functionally different for newcomers and seasoned practitioners alike.

When Gardner set down standards for modern *Wicca*, the practice of *Witchcraft* was still very much practiced in complete secrecy.* By its own definitions for *Initiation*: only a *Witch* could *Initiate* another *Witch.* And what's more, by the original classification of *coven*-structure, only a female (Priestess) could initiate a male (Priest) and only a male (Priest) could initiate a female (Priestess), except in the case of a parent and child. Treatment of gender in this respect is obviously not present in

---

* Anti-witchcraft laws are repealed in England in 1951.

"Dianic" traditions (which are exclusively female) and no longer appears to be a "typical" practice for *"New Age Wicca."*‡

Certainly, throughout history, there are many times when the existence of *Witchcraft* and other magical traditions is kept secret. In fact, under penalty of death, it was often necessary to do so. While membership of a *Coven* or *Grove* (or other "closed circles") is always to remain a privileged information, the basic knowledge of *Witchcraft* was also confined to personal apprenticeships and *Initiations* where a tradition could be passed on directly. Of course, until repeals of "Anti-witchcraft" laws—and even afterward—such a relationship required an outstanding measure of trust. Yet these days, widespread publishing of virtually *all* known materials has changed the game considerably.

INITIATION & THE WICCAN PATH

Many traditionalist still adhere to guidelines suggested in Gardner's *Book of Shadows*—but this standard is not directly applicable to solitary practitioners without modification; and we have seen a tremendous rise in "quiet solitaries" and even

---

‡ This is not a typical practice within the occult. Modern *Wicca* places a greater emphasis on distinguishing gender duality and its energetic reunion than most other "magical traditions."

those *Witches* that do converse with others, but remain unattached to a specific *Coven*. Changing laws, mass publication and increased public acceptance has also paved the way for more and more solo-newcomers to form their own *Covens* and *Groves*. Yet, when starting upon (or even rededicating one's attentions) to the *Wiccan Path*, whether alone or in a group, the fundamental applications of *Dedication* and *Initiation* remain to be handled.

Although all ritual applications produce their own quality of psychological effect on a practitioner, the practice of an *Initiation* is unique in being both a "magical ceremony" *and* "rite of passage."[†] This differs greatly from, for example, a "*spell*"—that is typically treated as "magick"—and from a "*Sabbat*" or "handfasting" (wedding)—considered primarily as a "rite of passage." A true *Initiation* demonstrates elements of both.

However, to be semantically clear of the distincti-

---

†   The term "Rite of Passage" is used in neopaganism to denote ceremonies observing a distinct "passage of time." Annually, this includes the eight seasonal "*Sabbats*" as the cycle-of-action reflected in Nature; for an individual during their lifetime, the traditional cycle-of-action is: birth/naming; coming-of-age; dedication; initiation; ordination; handfasting; birthing/"wiccaning"; and funerary.

on: a *Dedication* is a personal intentional act and "rite of passage," whereby an individual makes a firm decision to enter upon the *Wiccan Path.* This is a personal decision conducted on Self-determination alone; there are no other qualifiers or permissions required for this to occur. An individual can *Dedicate* themselves to the pursuit of a particular tradition on their own accord—or to the pursuit of a particular path presented by a certain *Coven, Grove* or organization. This is often treated as the "first step" towards "*Initiation.*"

Initiation differs from a *Dedication* in that it begins or "initiates" a *specific* cycle or period of work. In a *Coven* or group, the "rites of passage" are also intended to increase a close-knit relationship between membership of a similar knowledge base or degree/level of understanding. A structured methodology of *Initiation* is not unique only to *Witchcraft*; it may be found at the foundations of many other mystical orders and secret societies—from the "Freemasons" to the "Hermetic Order of the Golden Dawn."

Initiations represent a formal admittance into the group dynamic (or a certain "degree" or "level" of the group) when treated within a *Coven* or *Grove.* Such is intended to place attention or emphasis on the energetic harmony and security that follows with a sense of belonging and acceptance felt when participating in a group. The nature of the secrecy inherent in a *Coven*, and the freedom it provides the *Witch* in having a safe and open forum to communicate within, greatly resembles the qualities of a true "Socratic Society" referred to in the "*Pantheisticon*" of John Toland.[∞]

For longstanding organizations, there is also the matter of "Laying of Hands"—where an individual has had Power "passed" to them directly from a source; and they, in turn, dispense this further to others with physical contact. This manner of "anointing" may include ceremonial observance and oils, *&tc.*, but it can just as effective be performed by placing the open palm on top of someone's head and "willing" a transference by "intention."[‡]

"Rites of Initiation" appear in Gerald Gardner's *Book of Shadows* for "Three Degrees" of traditional *Witchcraft*, but most *Covens* and *Groves* choose to write their own unique versions—and most will not readily publish or release their full "Three Degrees of Initiation" to the "outer court" (meaning also what is readily available in bookstores) in or-

---

[∞] An annotated edition of John Toland's "*Pantheisticon*" (edited by Joshua Free) is available from the Systemology Society. It has since been reprinted in the Master Edition of "*Merlyn's Complete Book of Druidism*" and in the Mardukite Master Course "*Instructor's Manual*."

[‡] Or "prayer" by some semantic classifications.

der to retain an air of mystery over performance of the rites themselves—and also what each degree entails. This is a fundamental attribute of a graded "Mystery School" or "Initiatory Tradition."

"Rites of Initiation" are only participated in by those members that have already attained the degree that the initiate is being installed to. In some *Witchcraft* traditions, an initiate must study and practice within the degree they are installed to for "a year and a day" (366 days).[37] This would mean that at minimum, to receive formal "Ordination" as a *Priestess* or *Priest*, a *Witch* must work with a coven for a little over three years (1098 days).

"Ordained" *Priests* and *Priestesses* and other Elders compose an "Inner Circle" or "Inner Court"[*] that is responsible for continuing success and survival of the *Coven*. These individuals are also charged with the task of determining a gradient criteria for the Three Degree qualifications, the installation of novitiates to those degrees of the "Outer Court" and dispensing (teaching) the material. [Really, there are so many details to "coven

---

37 "Except in unusual cases, at least three of the *Witches* [from the "Inner Court"] must both privately and to the coven have vouched for the candidate... at lest three full moons must have passed between [levels] of initiation."—Ed Fitch, *A Grimoire of Shadows.*

* Possibly even to include "Third Degree" initiates.

craft" alone—enough to dedicate an entire book to
—but we have covered most of the necessary critical ground within the greater scope of *The Witch's
Handbook*.]

THE POWER OF INITIATION[‡]

Since the inception of the Ancient Mystery School
—stretching back on Earth's timeline into prehis-
tory—every esoteric tradition, spiritual system, religious sect, mystical order and secret society has
maintained one unique facet of "Self-Transformation" that has always proven quite effective when
properly understood and executed: *Initiation*.

For many individuals, the concept of *Initiation* is
reduced to antics of college fraternities (and soror-
ities), which employ facets and ideals of *Initiation*
to "imprint" the sense of "brotherhood" (or "sister-
hood") and "fellowship" on their members. It is
true that there is a "power" present when these
formal group indoctrinations take place—but there
is a deeper reason that they are effective, even if
much of the original purpose and symbolism has
since dissolved into obscurity.

When we examine "*Duncan's Monitor of Freemasonry*" and "*Complete System of Golden Dawn*

---

‡ Parts of this section reprinted in "*Crystal Clear*"
by Joshua Free.

Magic"—or even Gardner's "*Book of Shadows*," it is clear that "Rites of Initiation" are among the most colorful and widely published demonstrations of esoteric ceremony. They shine brightly in contrast to other more abstract philosophies and any underlying work that actually constitutes what a particular "degree" represents.

We can glance back into history; examining ancient Greek and Egyptian philosophical schools—now alluded to as Hermetic priesthoods and societies—not to mention the blatantly obvious demonstration of "*seven graded (tiered) initiation*" rituals observed in Mardukite Babylon; and everywhere else we find colorful depictions of "Rites of Initiation" prevalent in one or another form. For example: in ancient Europe, the Celtic Druids would lead initiates into caves—or blindfolded through elaborate labyrinths—to further demonstrate the "Journey of Self" successively reaching to higher and higher points on its Ascension.

The true purpose of *Initiation* is to "initiate" or "start" a new sequence or cycle-of-action. Mystical orders and secret societies maintain their own methods and terminology to *initiate* members; which is also why members are referred to as "*Initiates.*" Each point marked by an *Initiation* is both the "end of" and "start of" a cycle, "degree" or "level"—which denotes that a changed state or "transformation" has definitively occurred. If such a "shift" is not obvious to the *Witch*, then either the previous degree was not completed (or administered) properly, or the symbolism of the *Initiation* is not effectively relevant (or within the realm of present understanding and realizations).

Regardless of what type and flavor is evoked for an *Initiation*, the fundamental meaning behind such "Rites of Passage" remains the same: the death and reformation of the artificial; the shedding of old skin; and the rehabilitation of a clearer and greater, more widely encompassing, realization of *Self*—one step closer to its truest and highest state, sense of existence, or point-of-view. If the cycles of work and their dramatic representations in ceremony cannot accomplish this, the mode of play being taken in this Game is not truly effective as a "mysticism" or an "applied spiritual philosophy."

A true and effective "Rite of Initiation" requires more than a sequence of obscure actions and fancy words; it requires more than merely advancement to some new "title" or "rank" within a *coven* or social institution; requires far more than merely an ornately decorated setting, regalia and a lavish Temple. In fact, a truly effective "Rite of Initiation" requires none of these things mentioned. The most successfully employed "Rites of Initiation" must simply evoke effective symbolism and "presence" of the most important and powerful archetype of Self-transformation: death of the artificial self—the artificial personality.

THE PATH OF SELF-INITIATION[‡]

Originally, a practical revival of the *Witchcraft* tradition heavily depended on the *Coven*-unit and even its ability to network with other *Covens*. But regardless of whether or nor you formally decide to join (or develop) a *"Coven," "Circle"* or *"Grove"* of the *Wicca-Witchcraft* methodology— or by whatever name you choose to call such a close-knit "magical group"—a proper "Self-Dedication Rite" is really among the first true ritual operations performed by a modern *Witch*. This is a personal "solitary" occasion that is not dependent on any group—and in recent times, it has frequently substituted group-involvement altogether for those "flying solo."

Since the original customary traditions of *Wicca* all involved being "brought into the Craft" or "brought into the Circle" by a preexisting *Witch*, there is no emphasis on "Self-Dedication" in mid-20th Century *Gardnerian Wicca*. Within that same

---

‡ Parts of this section appear in *"Elvenomicon -or-Secret Traditions of Elves and Faeries: The Book of Elven Magick & Druid Lore"* by Joshua Free; reprinted in *"Merlyn's Complete Book of Druidism."*

framework, the idea of "Self-Initiation" is unheard of. This attitude became increasingly more relaxed in the 1970's, when other variations (highly influenced by Gardner's *Book of Shadows*) began to increase in membership—such as *Alexandrian Wicca* (propagated by Alex Sanders).

During the same decade, many also began publishing their *ye olde* "family traditions" and allegedly "hereditary" *Books of Shadows*—all of which have been determined to be remnants of Gardner's *Book of Shadows* and/or other elements of the "Magical Revival" taking place in the late 19th and early 20th Century.

This all being said: when it comes to *Wicca*, there are no texts for "Self-Initiation Rites" from antiquity—however, for the past several decades, and within other schools and paths, the idea of "Self-Dedication" and "Self-Initiation" is taken more seriously. Quite simply: independent practitioners have a greater access to resources—such as *this book*—than they did at the inception of modern Wicca. Therefore, the appearance of such material in contemporary "New Age" literature is a relatively recent addition.

To provide at least one example for our present purposes, the following "Self-Dedication Ceremony" is included for use by the "*Elven Fellowship Circle of Magick*" for official incorporation into the "*1998 Book of Shadows*." The text is originally intended for this unique brand of "Celtic Faerie Tradition *x* Druid Witchcraft," but the language may be amended and adapted for specific applications elsewhere. A variation of this rite appears in the original "*Elven-Faerie Grimoire*."‡ It may be performed without "elemental tools" and/ or as a sentiment of solidification after these are made and consecrated.

Focused meditation and "Self-Dedication Rites" performed in Nature may aid in bridging the relationship with the "natural," "spiritual"—or otherwise "metaphysical"—side of Reality. All magical prowess and ability is accumulated over time as a result of the good health and consistent growth of this relationship.

Communication in this relationship assists to break down the artificial barriers of fragmented separation between the *Self* and the *Universe*. What is considered "magical authority" or "occult power" is really derived from the ability to operate as *Self* in perfect clarity.*

For the "Rite of Self-Dedication," *cast* a *Witch's Circle* in the manner you have been instructed pre-

---

‡   See "*Elvenomicon*" by Joshua Free.
*   A concept referred to as "*Self-Honesty*" within the applied spiritual philosophies of "*Mardukite Systemology*."

viously—even if you have only envisioned doing so in your mind as you read *The Witch's Handbook* (because "imagination" is a form of magic itself, when the energy is properly directed). Have an "elemental candle" placed at each direction (if possible) before energetically tracing the boundary of the Magic Circle by hand (or by *Wand*).

Once the area is consecrated as "sacred space," go to the center of the Magic Circle—you do not necessarily need an *Altar* for this rite—and stand (or kneel), facing north, saying:

> "In my mortal form I am known as [*your given name*], but today [*tonight*] I come to you in my true$^\infty$ form with the name [*chosen magical name*]. Spirits of the Universe, I approach you not as [*former name*] but as the Witch† [*new name*]."

Take a *Bowl of Salt* and remove a pinch, placing it on your tongue. Get the sense of the Earth elemental energy flowing through the body, then say:

> "I am a Child of Earth; I am a Child of the Stars. I have studied the Way in preparation

---

∞ Originally given as "*Elven-Ffayrie*."

$\dagger$ Originally given as "*Elf-Child*"; or "*Ffayrie-Child*" for females; or "*Elf-Friend*" for mortal practitioners uncertain of their personal involvement with the Elven-Faerie legacy on Earth.

but now I seek the Spirits of Nature to be my teacher—my instructor in the true mystic sciences of the Cosmos. O Great Spirits of the Universe, hidden in your fold likes the question and answer of Creation and Life, which is one and the same. We are One—and I am one with the entire Universe, seeking to share a communication with All."

Stand and move to the north and light the green "elemental candle," saying:

"Spirits of the Enchanted Forest, of plants and rocks and trees, awaken and know me as [*magical name*]. I come to this Magic Circle with peace within, in perfect love and perfect trust, and seek your aid in learning your mysteries. I vow this day [*night*] to ever uphold thy secrets, to ever walk the path of wisdom, and to ever share the illumination of enlightenment. Hear me, for I am a follower of the Wiccan Ways."√

Trace a symbol, "seal" or personal "sigil" representative of the Earth Element that you will use regularly in your rites to incite energetic activity *of* the Earth Element in the north. Traditionally examples include elemental "pentagrams" or other

---

√ Originally given as "*Elven Way.*"

"signs of portal."[38] Envision this "Sign of Earth" as green in color, then speak:

> "By this sign shall we know each other."

Move to the east and light the yellow "elemental candle," saying:

> "Spirits of the Enchanted Breeze, of winds and sky and Air, awaken and know me as [*magical name*]. I come to this Magic Circle with peace within, in perfect love and perfect trust, and seek your aid in learning your mysteries. I vow this day [*night*] to ever uphold thy secrets, to ever walk the path of wisdom, and to ever share the illumination of enlightenment. Hear me, for I am a follower of the Wiccan Ways."

Trace your "sigil" representing the "Sign of Air" and see it yellow as you speak:

> "By this sign shall we know each other."

Go to the south, lighting the red "elemental candle," and say:

> "Spirits of the Enchanted Mountain, of sun

---

38 This line refers directly to illustrations and instructions given in "*The Sorcerer's Handbook*" (and also reprinted in *The Great Magickal Arcanum*).

and star and flame, awaken and know me
as [*magical name*]. I come to this Magic
Circle with peace within, in perfect love
and perfect trust, and seek your aid in
learning your mysteries. I vow this day
[*night*] to ever uphold thy secrets, to ever
walk the path of wisdom, and to ever share
the illumination of enlightenment. Hear
me, for I am a follower of the Wiccan
Ways."

Trace your "sigil" for the "Sign of Fire," seeing it
red, and speaking:

"By this sign shall we know each other."

Move to the west and light the blue "elemental
candle," saying:

"Spirits of the Enchanted Sea, of wave and
lake and rain, awaken and know me as
[*magical name*]. I come to this Magic
Circle with peace within, in perfect love
and perfect trust, and seek your aid in
learning your mysteries. I vow this day
[*night*] to ever uphold thy secrets, to ever
walk the path of wisdom, and to ever share
the illumination of enlightenment. Hear
me, for I am a follower of the Wiccan
Ways."

Trace your "sigil" representing the "Sign of Water," and see it blue as you speak:

"By this sign shall we know each other."

Return to the center and take some anointing oil—
a type of your own personal choosing.[39] The Magical Traditions teach to "anoint" with oil from the
feet to the head (upward); and bless or wash from
head to foot (downward). Therefore, begin by
anointing your feet and say:

"Blessed be the feet that bring me here this
day [*night*] and enable me to touch the
ground, to walk the Path of the Ancients,
treading the Right Way always; never devi-
ating from the ascending path of true enlightenment and wisdom."

Anoint your knees, saying:

"Blessed be the knees that bend to give reverence to the Higher Power of the Universe

---

39 The original edition eliminated any further
suggestion here, although in the 1999 installment
of "*Crystalline Awakening*" the author clarified
that ancient pagans and *Witches* used a type of
"Flying Ointment" during these rites, composed
of substances and herbs that could be considered
toxic, hallucinogenic or illegal in various areas.
But, for academic purposes, most surviving
recipes include: belladonna, betel, cannabis,
datura, hemlock, henbane, opium and wolfbane.

to the Source of All Being in the Cosmos that gives me the strength to move forth on the ascending path of Light and the ability to make or break my stride at Will."

Anoint the palms of each hand and say:

"Blessed be the hands that lift in praise of the Universe and all Life. They are my commanding hands that I raise in power and I acknowledge their ability to direct my Will, as they are extensions of my creative mind."

Anoint the heart (left breast), saying:

"Blessed be the flame that burns strongly in my heart, that I may experience and know the True Love of the Universe, and in so doing, that I may recognize the Right Way by what is sensed deeply burning within my Spirit."

Anoint your lips and say:

"Blessed be the lips that speak the sacred words of incantation. May the words they speak only advance my evolution further on the ascending path, and never idle or in vain. From my mouth, I utter the Words of Power and share in the Breath of the All; yet I remain silent to those who do not know."

Finally, speak the following as you anoint your forehead:

> "Blessed be the mind that seeks to understand its own nature and its connection to the True Self; the Mind that allows me the ability to communicate true knowledge and guidance from Self to this Body—which is connected by the Mind. Let my thoughts be pure and of only a nature that will move me forward on the pathway of my Ascension."

It is traditional to "dedicate" (and ritually "consecrate" if possible) an item—traditionally a *Pendant*—that signifies and solidifies the personal dedication and commitment to the Path expressed in this rite; and of course, is later worn as continuing representation of the same. It is very common for a *Witch* to select the "pentagram" or "pentacle" for this pendant, although this is not a strict criteria.* If you are skilled in "Rites of Consecration" then do so; otherwise, simply hold up your talisman and say:

> "May the Spirits of Nature, the Cosmos and Universal Ocean beyond, witness and bless

---

* In the original "Elven-Faerie Druid" tradition this rite is derived from, it is more common to select a "septagram" or "seven-pointed star" (otherwise known as an "Elf Star" or "Faerie Star").

this symbol of my dedication. Recognize
this symbol and me, so that we may know
each other in our future exchanges."

To complete the ceremony, thank and cordially
dismiss all energies called to the rite and extinguish the Magic Circle.

THREE DEGREES OF INITIATION

The subject of qualifying requirements for defining a *"First Degree Witch"* (&tc.) from other degrees has been ambiguous since the inception of
modern *Witchcraft* traditions—for while many
may argue otherwise, there are essentially no "universal" designations set down in Gardner's *Book
of Shadows* or anywhere else in antiquity for that
matter, when pertaining specifically to *"Witchcraft."*

Given the background of its modern founder (or
compiling publicist) and the relationship of *"English Witchcraft"* with other local esoteric movements, it is, of course, easy to draw obvious paral-
lels between *Wicca* and degrees of "Druidism"
(which are *Ovate*, *Bardd* and *Derwydd*); and even
the most commonly observed master degrees of a
"Masonic blue lodge" (of which there are three).

Initiation scripts from the *Book of Shadows* intro-
duce (or indoctrinate) the *Witch* (initiate) to a

standard of group dynamics coupled with "degrees" or gradients of experience, learning and practice—the extent of which has continued to grow more diverse in today's society, as increasingly more material and "personal traditions" are incorporated into the wide encompassing body of potential "*Wiccan*" and "*spell*" literature on the market today.

Prior to mass circulation of Gardner's original *Book of Shadows*, what many "founding authorities" would later present could only demonstrate just how far they had, themselves, reached in a preexisting group (that may or may not have been closer to a "source" for the tradition) before branching off to form their own *covens*.[‡] The truth is: schisms of leadership and other issues are just as common in neopaganism as any other organizational system or institution—in spite of all the talk of "equality" and "acceptance" on the surface.

Traditionally, an *initiate Witch* is given official "charge" of their tools (or having tools they have made be ceremonially returned to them, once they are consecrated by the *High Priestess*, or an administrative leader of the group) at the "First Degree Initiation."

One common requirement for attaining "Second Degree" is to conduct an "original" *Esbat* ("Full

---

‡   This was once an issue with *Alexandrian Wicca*.

Moon Rite") for the *Coven*; and an "original" *Sabbat* ("Seasonal Rite") for the "Third Degree."[∞] A possible prerequisite for "Ordination"[†] might be performing and directing a group spellworking. Of course, this criteria is not set in stone; but the suggestion demonstrates an ascending gradient for practical understanding of *Witchcraft*.

∞ In 1998-1999, the first three degrees of the *Elven Fellowship Circle of Magick* were distinguished by: a demonstrable understanding of "pagan/Wiccan" religion and "seasonal" practices (*First Degree*); a demonstrable understanding of "ritual magick" and "spellcraft" (*Second Degree*); and a demonstrable understanding of "ceremonial magick" (*Third Degree*). [The modern *Mardukite Academy* observes the "Three Grades" entirely different for the *Mardukite Master Course*.]

† There are some traditionalist perspectives of *Witchcraft* that view *all* initiates as "Priests" or "Priestesses"—as in *every Wiccan* is considered "clergy." This extends back to the idea of *Witchcraft* as a rebellion to the Church, where parishioners are reliant on "intermediary clergy" for their connection with the "Divine." In more modern applications, a "*Third Degree Witch*" may opt to become "ordained" with full ministerial licensing to not only lead a *coven* but other *legal* sanctions (wedding services, &tc.) just as other "recognized clergy" when registered properly with applicable states, &tc.

We will treat the subject of *Gardnerian Initiations* later on in this notebook, but for present purposes, it is most important to illustrate "Rites of Initiation" as they are actually practiced by the *Elven Fellowship Circle of Magick* and its prospective developments into the *Order of the Crystal Dawn.**

NEOPHYTE—FIRST DEGREE INITIATION§

To be considered for membership into *Coven*, and *Initiation* into each subsequent *Degree*, a candidate must be "sponsored" by a referral from a member in good standing, which is also responsible for securing a majority vote on this action from existing members. The "Sponsor" must also be present at the *Initiation* (or *Installation*) ceremony.

---

*   Original circulation of this "*Sorcerer's Notebook*" ("*Witch's Handbook*") in 1998-1999 was restricted to members of groups involved with or networking with Joshua Free (as "Merlyn Stone"). Portions of it later appeared in *The Great Magickal Arcanum* and *Elvenomicon*.

§   As modified from the "*1998 Book of Shadows.*" Parts of this section appear in "*Elvenomicon -or- Secret Traditions of Elves and Faeries: The Book of Elven Magick & Druid Lore*" by Joshua Free; reprinted in "*Merlyn's Complete Book of Druidism.*" During the late 1990's, this rite was practiced publicly a dozen times in "Washington Park" (Denver, Colorado).

Such group ceremonies or *coven* gatherings are only open to those members already initiated to the *Degree* (or above) that the Magic Circle is operated for.[‡]

The "Sponsor" leads a *blindfolded* "Initiate" to the northeast corner of the Magic Circle, where they are met by the "Guardian of the Grove" (which may also be the "Leader") standing at the boundary holding a sword. [In some versions, the hands of the "Initiate" are also bound behind their back; the ends of a cord are tied to each ankle, permitting the "Initiate" to walk freely without injury, but not necessarily "run."] Although a "Guardian" may always be "at arms" to protect the *Coven*, the later subsequent (standard) admissions into a "Circle of the First Degree" [also known as the "*Rite of the Blade*" or "*Passing the Kiss*"] are conducted with an *Athame*, or black-handled *Dagger.*

Guardian: "Who is it there that you
                      bring here to the very
                      Gates of this Sphere
                      most Sacred and
                      Secret?"

[‡]   With the exception of *Initiations* and certain
       levels of group "spellwork," a typical operating
       Circle for a *Coven* (group) is "cast" or "sealed"
       by the "First Degree"—such as for *Esbats* and
       Sabbats when participation by all members is
       encouraged.

Sponsor:	"I bring a Child of Earth and Star. They come seeking entrance; to be set on the Pathway of our Mysteries."
Guardian:	"Do you then present this person to the *Coven*,[∞] vouching before us for their conduct and their dedication to our circle and the Wiccan Ways?"[√]
Sponsor:	"I do. I sponsor this Child of Earth and Star and take responsibility for them as they enter the Gates of this Sphere most Sacred and Secret. They remain outside the Circle now, in a state of darkness—blinded to the mysteries of our Sphere."
Guardian:	"Then as Guardian of this Gateway and Keeper of this Sphere, I open the Portal to our Magic

---

∞ Originally given as "*Grove*."
√ Originally given as "*Elven Ways*."

> Circle with this Sword. I
> permit you to enter this
> one time only by the Un
> speakable Password."[†]

The "Sponsor" leads the "Initiate" to the center of
the Magic Circle, where they stand before the
"Leader" (or *High Priestess*) and encircled by the
existing membership of the *Coven*.

Leader: "I address the Initiate to answer—
Do you come here seeking en
trance to our *Coven?*

Initiate: "I do."

Leader: "Answer, Initiate—Do you come
here of your own free will, free
from the pressures of peers or others and free of ulterior motives or
malevolent infiltration?"

Initiate: "I do."

Leader: "And one more, Initiate, answer
—Are you willing to submit to an
oath of secrecy sworn by the ancient covenant of Witches,[*] before

---

[†] The Magic Circle, being previously "Cast" by
existing members, is energetically "cut open" in
the shape of a "Doorway" with the *Blade* and
then resealed with an opposite motion.

[*] Originally given as "*by the ancient covenant of
the Mystic Wizards of the Earth and this*

the members of the Coven and the
Spirits we have called to this
Magic Circle?"

Initiate: "I do."

Leader: "Then kneel and submit yourself
to this Assembly."

The "Sponsor" may assist the "Initiate" to kneel
and then joins the outer circle of members. These
encircling members begin to "murmur and whisper" softly as they rotate their position clockwise
around the boundary of the Magic Circle. The
"Leader" (or *High Priestess*) speaks the following
passage while circling closely around the "Initiate"
counter-clockwise.

Leader: "You have entered a place that is
not a place; a time that is not a
time; and still you are here. You
have entered the Deep Woods and
found yourself in the Enchanted
Forest of the Elves and Faerie un
solicited. You step foot on ground
held most sacred to the Keepers
of the Earth; those that maintain
and celebrate the Ancient Ways.
Under penalty of death, no mortal
shall step foot in our Kingdom
unbidden, and thus you not render
yourself to the mercy of this

Council."

Court. Fear has no place here in
the Otherworld—and it is the will
of this court that you be sentenc-
ed to death if you now enter this
place without the passwords. If
you bring mortal fear in your
heart to our world, you will surely
summon your demises. So, I ask
you again, Initiate—how do you
seek to enter our world?"[40]

The final line is asked with the "Leader" (or *High Priestess*) standing in front of the "Initiate," at which time the surrounding motions and murmuring ceases. The "Sponsor" also returns to the side of the "Initiate."

Initiate: "With the passwords—*perfect love* and *perfect trust*."

Leader: "I address the Sponsor to answer —has the Initiate been properly prepared? Have they completed their Self-Dedication to our ways? Are they recognized by the Elemental Watchtowers?"

Sponsor: "The Initiate is prepared. They are properly dedicated. They are

40 This passage is based heavily on the records of Rev. Robert Kirk; see "*Elvenomicon*" by Joshua Free, also reprinted in "*Merlyn's Complete Book of Druidism.*"

        recognized by the Elemental
        Realms."

Leader: "We shall find out... May the
        Source of All Being and Creation
        grant us protection; and in protec-
        tion, strength; and in strength,
        peace; and in peace, understand-
        ing; and in understanding, know-
        ledge; and in knowledge, wisdom;
        and in wisdom, love; and in love,
        the love of all things; and in the
        love of all things, the love of all
        the Universe and Creation...‡ The
        Initiate may rise."

The "Sponsor" summons the "Initiate" up from their knees, then guides them on a cross-quarter journey to the various "elemental directions" in the Magic Circle before returning them to the center again. In ancient times, this would have been conducted in a cave or labyrinth.

The following ritual text[41] is read by the "Leader" (or *High Priestess*) on one side of the "Initiate,"

---

‡ This passage is known as the "*Druid's (Gorsedd) Prayer.*"

41 The ritual text is based heavily on the "Chaldean Oracles of Zoroaster" (as given in the "*Anunnaki Bible*"), which were also used as inspiration by the Hermetic Order of the Golden Dawn for their "Watchtower Ceremony."

while movement around the Circle is led by the "Sponsor" from the other side.

South: "In the Beginning was the Infinite Void of Nothingness—a canvas with no form, a screen without picture. But then came Light; the Dragon; the Cosmic Law—that which gave all existence its form; waves of potentiality sprawling across the matrix-fabric of the Universe as the Fires of Life."

East: "And when the Fires of Life burned down to glowing embers, they breathed existence into the Air—they breathed the knowledge and Life into the Air; and was born the Spirits[∞] of the Breeze."

West: "Then more and more tangible did the formless Spirit of Light become. When the Waters emerged, its ripples were sent out to every corner of existence as an All-Encompassing Sea. But the waves and currents of energy chased one another and became even more solid."

North: "So, the Formless Fire gave birth

∞   Originally given as "*Elves, Ffayrie and Sylphs.*"

to Air; the gaseous Air gave way to Water—the Sea would yield finally to the Land, the Element of Earth; a powerfully strong and stable foundation to solidly hold up the less tangible manifestations. The Earth is home to the planetary Spirit of G'ea.√ She has had 'Keepers' and 'Guardians' at all times, and in all places, to maintain the balance of the Elemental World and thwart all that would cause disharmony to Life on Earth and in the Cosmos."

Center: "As you have come to us in the darkness of ignorance, know that we are the 'Keepers of the Earth', the 'Guardians of the Green World' and 'Scions of the Secret Knowledge' kept since the times of the Ancient Mystery School. [*Removes blindfold from "Initiate."*] As you emerge, reborn into a Realm of Light and our world of enchantment, your given name is no longer appropriate and is retired at the boundary of the Magic Circle.† By what name shall this

---

√   Also "*Gaia*" or "*Gaea*."
†   Originally given as "*Sacred Grove.*"

> *Coven* know you as?"

Initiate: [*Answers.*]

Leader: "Then, Lords and Ladies of this
Coven, I present to you our new
Initiate, [*name*]. We welcome
them into our Magic Circle as a
Free Person."[*]

APPRENTICE—SECOND DEGREE INITIATION[§]

The "Second Degree Initiation" used by the *Elven Fellowship Circle of Magick* is otherwise known as the "*Rite of the Law*"—part of which is standard for sealing a "Circle of the Second Degree" (coupled with the "*Rite of the Blade*" and "*Passing the*

---

[*] Each of the members, starting with the Leader, formally greets the Initiate by name "as a Free Person." In some "Gardnerian" inspired versions, the Leader (or *High Priestess*) would also entrust the "Third Password" to the Initiate, which is "*a kiss.*" [The first two passwords are "*perfect love*" and "*perfect trust.*"]

[§] As given in the "*1998 Book of Shadows.*" Parts of this section appear in the "Appendix" to the 21st Anniversary Collector's Edition "*Sorcerer's Handbook*" by Joshua Free (writing as Merlyn Stone).

Kiss"). The *Rite of Initiation* is, itself, only one part of achieving the actualized state of "Awakened Apprentice."

In some versions, the "Initiate" is placed in a wooden *Coffin* or alone in a *Crypt* for a period of time prior to any ceremonial performance or interaction. Such "introspection" is meant for an "Initiate" to overcome "reactivity" to personal "programming" and any "mental imagery" that is conjured to mind as a result—all of which must be "worked out," until the "Initiate" is sufficiently "emptied."‡

Historically, this has also left things open for abuses and other mishandling, because an individual may also need to resolve "panic responses" to feeling that the "body" is trapped; when the realization intended here is for *Self* as *Spirit* to realize they are not restricted to the *Body*, and in essence, become free of these considerations. It is not uncommon to experience *Self* apart from the *Body* during this exercise.

When practiced alone, an "Initiate" may simply choose to isolate away reclusive for a time; making sure to have minimal stimuli in the environment—clearing out a special room or covering up

---

‡ For additional information on this type of energy work, refer to "*The Tablets of Destiny*" and "*Crystal Clear*" by Joshua Free.

shelving and furniture around the house. During deep periods of this work, no electronic devices or artificial lighting is permitted; and a dietary fasting on breads and water is encouraged. While many elements discussed in this section of *The Witch's Handbook* may seem extreme, I would invite readers to also consider the preparatory purification work suggested in the text: *Sacred Magic of Abramelin the Mage.*[∞]

Ancient records and accounts of *True Initiation Rites* do not give the type of detailed descriptions of ritual instruction and ceremonial verbiage is taken for granted today in the "New Age"—since the magical revival of the late 1800's or even the reconstruction of *Freemasonry* in 1717. In an archaic account by W. Winwood Reade—"*The Veil of Isis -or- Mysteries of the Druids*"—we are given at least one amazing perspective on the awesome symbolism and power of imagination in connection to *Initiations* of the Ancient Mystery School:

> "*During a period of probation, the Ovate was closely watched; eyes, to him, invisible, were ever upon him, noting his actions and his very looks, searching into his heart for its motive, and into his soul for its abilities. He was then subjected to a trial so painful to the body, so terrible to the*

[∞] For details, refer to "*The Great Magickal Arcanum*" by Joshua Free.

mind, that any lost their senses for ever, and others crawled back to the daylight pale and emaciated, as men who had grown old in prison.

"These initiations took place in caves, one of which still exists in Denbighshire. We have also some reason to believe that the catacombs of Egypt and those artificial excavations which are to be found in many parts of Persia and Hindostan were constructed for the same purpose.

"The Ovate received several wounds from a man who opposed his entrance with a drawn sword. He was then led blindfolded through the winding alleys of the cave which was also a labyrinth. This was meant to represent the toilsome wanderings of the soul in the mazes of ignorance and vice. Presently the ground would begin to rock beneath his feet; strange sounds disturbed the midnight silence. Thunder crashed upon him like the fall of an avalanche, flashes of green lightning flickered through the cave displaying to his view hideous spectres arrayed against the walls.

"Then lighted only by these fearful fires, a strange procession marched past him, and a hymn in honor of the Eternal Truth was

solemnly chanted by unseen tongues. Here the profounder mysteries commenced. He was admitted through the North Gate or that of Cancer, where he was forced to pass through a Wall of Fire. Thence he hurried to the Southern Gate or that of Capricorn, where he was plunged into a flood, and from which he was only released when life was at its last gasp. Then he was scourged and buried up to his neck in snow. This was the baptism by fire, of water and of blood.

"*Now arrived on the verge of death, an icy chill seizes his limbs; a cold dew bathes his brow, his faculties fail him; his eyes close; he is about to faint, to expire, when a strain of music, sweet as the distant murmur of the holy brooks, consoling as an angel's voice, bids him to rise and to live for the honor of his God. Two doors with a sound like the fluttering of wings are thrown open before him. A divine light bursts upon him, he sees plains shining with flowers open around him.*

"*Then a golden serpent is placed in his bosom as a sign of his regeneration, and he is adorned with a mystic zone upon which are engraved twelve mysterious signs; a tiara is placed on his head; his form naked and shivering is clothed in a purple tunic*

> *studded with innumerable stars; a crozier is placed in his hand... He is a king; for he is initiated; for he is a Druid."*

Returning to our practical application: if some method of "solitary confinement" has been applied, then the "Leader" (or *High Priestess*) is responsible for opening the door or coffin-cover for the "initiate" and welcoming them into the Magic Circle (or lodge, as this *Rite* was originally conducted indoors). However, it is not always possible for the formerly described "*Awakening Rite*" to precede the ceremony; in which case, the "Initiate" is blindfolded with their hands bound behind them —as is customary for all *Rites of Initiation*.

Second-Degree and Third-Degree members wait within the Magic Circle, properly prepared according to the Grade of *Installation* (and the "Sponsor" begins among them). The "Leader" (the "Master of the Craft" or *High Priestess*) stands in the center; the "Guardian" waits at the door (or northeast threshold) with drawn sword; the "Initiate" is left waiting outside the door to the lodge (or some distance away from the Circle or Grove).

Guardian:	"Master of the Craft, I come with news of an Initiate awaiting entrance into the *Second*

Degree of our *Coven*."[√]

Leader:	"Who accounts for this candidate?"
Sponsor:	"I do. They stand outside the Magic Circle seeking entrance to the *Second Degree*."
Leader:	"Is the candidate properly prepared for the *Second Degree*?"
Sponsor:	"They are."
Leader:	"Then I permit you to break circle and accompany the Guard to see that the candidate is properly prepared for this installation ceremony."

The "Sponsor" and "Guard" go and prepare the "Initiate" for the ceremony, bringing them to the door of the lodge or northeast boundary of the Magic Circle.

The password for admittance to the *Second Degree* is a "knock" sequence: 1-2-3 or /-//-///. This is traditionally done on the door to a ceremonial cha-

---

[√] Originally given as "*our Sacred Order*," in preparation for continued use by the *Order of the Crystal Dawn*.

mber, though when conducted outdoors, an artificial "knocker" or "clacker"[†] is used, or even a bell.

The "Guard" then opens the door (and "cuts the doorway" for the Circle as previously described) and announces to the *Coven.*

Guardian:	"I return with the Initiate and their Sponsor."
Leader:	"Is the Initiate properly prepared?"
Sponsor:	"They are."
Leader:	"Then bring them forward and let the installation ceremony commence. Guard, seal the Doorway to this Magic Circle and let no one interfere with these operations."
Guardian:	"The Magic Circle is sealed."
Leader:	"Then we may proceed.

---

† A wooden "Clacker" (a hammer-like piece strikes a board) or "Clapper" (thin boards slap against a center board) is still used in some churches today in place of bells during lent—particularly the Easter Triduum of Holy Week. The correct term within the Roman Catholic Church is "*crotalus*" (Latin) from the Greek "*krotalon*" ("rattle").

Sponsor—you may present your candidate for initiation."

Sponsor: "Master of the Craft, it is my honor to present this candidate for initiation to the *Second Degree* of our *Coven*. I petition this assembly to allow this candidate installation to the *Second Degree* of this *Coven*, and mark its occasion."

Leader: "Let the candidate speak for themselves, now. Initiate—what do you come here seeking from us?"

Initiate: [*Answers.*]

Leader: "Initiate—is there any reason why you would be unable to submit yourself to the confidence and commitment of this Assembly at this time?"

Initiate: [*Answers.*]

Leader: "Fine. Thank you. Then, I address the Assembly —is there any member

of this *Coven* that does
not believe this candid-
ate is worthy of the
Second Degree?"

Respondents: [*Answer, if applicable.*]

Leader: "Then if there will be no
objections, it is with
great pleasure and es-
teem that we elevate and
install you [*name of
candidate*] to the *Second
Degree* of the [*name of
Coven or group*]. By the
reputation of your Spon-
sor and on the recom-
mendation of this Ass-
embly, we are assured
that you are befitting of
the *Second Degree*
among *Witches*,[*] and that
you fully understand the
sacred trust bestowed on
you by this fellowship.
Those who come to this
fellowship in Self-Hon-
esty seek to be Self-
Masters; assisting them-

---

[*] Originally given as "*Brothers and Sisters of this
lodge.*"

selves and assisting others to assist themselves on the Pathway to Ascension. Initiate—do you understand all of what I have said?"

Initiate: [*Answers.*]

Leader: "To be an integral part of this *Coven*‡ is to seek Self-Honesty, Universal Truth, and the power laden in both. We seek to understand the true nature and potential of the Human Condition, now waiting to be unlocked within you. You are here this day to reconfirm your place on the Pathway to Ascension, the quest for ultimate potential and the promise of its loftiest uses, affirming that the Spark of the Divine is within you—and that Humans are not Animals. Initiate—are you

---

‡   Originally given as "*Sacred Order.*"

able to solidify this
commitment here before
your *Coven*?"

Initiate: [*Answers.*]

Leader: "The Sponsor may remove the bindings from
this Initiate; in doing so,
know that you are now
unbound to the potential
of the *Second Degree*,
free to pursue its teach-
ings and receive its
instruction from this
Coven."

The Sponsor removes the bindings from the Initiate.

Leader: "The Sponsor may remove the
blindfold from this Initiate; in doing so, know that you are now
seeing the light of this *Coven's*
Second Degree for the first time.
With new eyes you are free to see
and realize its teachings and the
actualized potential within yourself in Self-Honesty. One cannot
seek what they cannot see."

The Sponsor removes the blindfold from the Initiate and greets them as a "Free Person of the
Second Degree"; after which each members of the

Coven also comes up to do the same before returning to the Assembly.

> Leader: "We officially declare [*name*] a Free Person initiated to the *Second Degree*. Initiate—you may now join the greater Assembly of this *Coven*, gathered together to affirm the Law given to those that Ascend the Pathway."

The Initiate joins the Assembly for the remainder of the ceremony, which is the "*Rite of the Law*."[42]

> Leader: "Some want to watch the things that move. Some want to tear with teeth and claws. Some go out in the world, fighting. Some go out biting. Punishment is sharp and sure for those who act against the Law. You have heard of the Law of the Jungle; but we follow the Law of the Highest! A Human is not an Animal. Man is not an Animal. Today, I am the Sayer of

---

42 Versions of this rite were popularized as "*TierDrama*" in the 1960's-70's by those employing "*Satanic Rituals*" of Anton LaVey, where it is presented under the premise of a 1776 Bavarian Illuminati ritual. The text is more likely derived from its appearance in the 1896 novel by H.G. Wells titled: "*The Island of Dr. Moreau*."

the Law. Speak the words and
learn the Law! Not to go on all
fours; this is the Law."

Respondents: "Not to go on all fours;
that is the Law."

Leader: "Not to tear at plants and trees;
this is the Law."

Respondents: "Not to tear at plants
and trees; that is the
Law."

Leader: "Not to snarl and roar; this is the
Law."

Respondents: "Not to snarl and roar;
that is the Law."

Leader: "Not to show teeth or fangs; this
is the Law."

Respondents: "Not to show teeth or
fangs; that is the Law."

Leader: "Not to destroy our possessions
or habitats; this is the Law."

Respondents: "Not to destroy our
possessions or habitats;
that is the Law."

Leader: "Not to kill without thought; this
is the Law."

Respondents: "Not to kill without
thought; that is the
Law."

Leader: "Humans are God."

Respondents: "Humans are God."

Leader: "We are Human."

Respondents: "We are Human."

Leader: "We are Gods."

Respondents: "We are Gods."

Leader: "Ours is the hand that creates; this is the Law."

Respondents: "Ours is the hand that creates; that is the Law."

Leader: "Ours is the hand that wounds; this is the Law."

Respondents: "Ours is the hand that wounds; that is the Law."

Leader: "Ours is the hand that heals; this is the Law."

Respondents: "Ours is the hand that heals; that is the Law."

Leader: "Ours is the lightning flash; this is the Law."

Respondents: "Ours is the lightning flash; that is the Law."

Leader: "Ours is the deep salty sea; this is the Law."

Respondents: "Ours is the deep salty sea; that is the Law."

Leader: "Ours is the stars in the sky; this is the Law."

Respondents: "Ours is the stars in the sky; that is the Law."

Leader: "Ours is the rulers of the land; this is the Law."

Respondents: "Ours is the rulers of the land; that is the Law."

Leader: "This is what is ours to have; this is what we are."

Respondents: "This is what is ours to have; this is what we are."

Leader: "The Rite of the Law is ended, but its truth ever remains. Blessed Be."[∞]

Respondents: "Blessed Be All."

For "Outer Court" purposes, this "*Rite of Initiation*" may also be amended for installation to a *Third Degree*.[√]

[∞] Originally given as "*So Mote it Be.*"

[√] Additional suggestions may be found in the Appendix of the 21st Anniversary Collector's Edition of "*The Sorcerer's Handbook*" by Joshua Free writing as Merlyn Stone. Note the details for "Installation of a Master," which is dependent on knowledge and experience with ceremonial arts described in that volume. The "*1998 Book of*

THE GARDNERIAN INITIATIONS

Many versions of *Initiation* are presented by Gerald Gardner during his lifetime, with later modifications provided by Doreen Valiente. Original "Gardnerian Initiations" are a staple of *Wiccan* foundations for not only Gardnerian traditions, but much of the popular *Witchcraft* that came afterward—new traditions frequently based on "word-of-mouth" versions of the same *Book of Shadows*, by those who had actually participated in Gardnerian *Covens*. In modern times, given how widespread the *Book of Shadows* has reached, any "Mystery" surrounding *Initiation* through "three degrees of *Witchcraft*" has been all but threshed out. Most *Covens* have since opted to write completely different *Rites of Initiation*, such as seen above.*

Shadows" (now "*The Witch's Handbook*") was intended primarily for "Outer Court" (training coven) use; and secondly, for incorporation with the original "*Sorcerer's Handbook*"—along with "*Draconomicon*" and its follow up "*Druid's Handbook*"—which, when combined together, represent the complete "Third Degree" ("Master") library established during the "Merlyn Stone" period from 1995 until 2000. This collection of materials later constituted the core of *The Great Magickal Arcanum*, first released in 2008.

* This section regarding *Gardnerian Initiation* contains some material never officially practiced

In descriptions for "*First Degree Initiation,*" the "Initiate" (referred to as the "Postulant") is cable-towed to the edge of the Magic Circle. There hands are bound with a red cord that is also around the neck—a practice that would be perhaps ill-advised today. The "Initiator" commands that the "feet be neither bound nor free," which is a strange instruction, worked out as described in a previous section above. In another version, a short cord is attached to the right ankle, and another just below the right knee.

One interesting characteristic of early *Gardnerian Wicca* is the inclusion of the "Kabbalistic Cross" during the Opening Rites, commonly used in Jewish mysticism and by the Golden Dawn magicians —and given in the text of *The Sorcerer's Handbook*. However, during the "*Rite of Initiation,*" the Magic Circle is left "open" at the northeast threshold, where the "Postulant" stands just outside of it in wait; their "Sponsor" standing behind them. Otherwise, the Magic Circle is "cast" in the usual manner.

Another significant facet is the "*Rite of the Blade,*" where the "Initiator" approaches the "Postulant" standing outside the Magic Circle and says: "*You who stands on the threshold between the pleasant*

---

by the *Elven Fellowship Circle of Magick;* it is included here only for academic purposes and posterity.

world of men and the dread domains of the Lords of the Outer Spaces, do you have the courage to attempt to enter this Circle?"

The "Initiator" then places the point of the *Blade* against the Postulant's chest, continuing: *"For I say verily, it were better to rush upon my blade and perish, then make the attempt with fear in your heart."* And the "Postulant" responds: *"I have two passwords: Perfect Love and Perfect Trust."*

When the "Initiate/Postulant" is finally brought into the Magic Circle, the "Leader/Initiator" (or *High Priestess*) entrusts the "Third Password" (a "*kiss*"), then comes around to behind the "Postulant" with their embrace as they nudge/thrust them into the Circle.

The purpose of this is described in Gerald Gardner's novel "*High Magic's Aid*," where an *Witch* is questioned by outsiders with: "Who led you into the Circle?"—and the appropriate answer, being: "They led me from behind." Once inside the Circle, the Postulant is escorted to (and announced before) each ritual station of the Elemental directions—"Take heed, Lords of the Watchtower of the East, that [*so-and-so*] is properly prepared to be initiated a *Witch* and *Priestess* [*or Priest*], &tc."

Once brought to the center of the Magic Circle, existing *Coven* members begin to circle around *deosil* (sun-wise, clock-wise), chanting: *"Eko, Eko, Azarak; Eko, Eko, Zomelak; Eko, Eko, Kernunnos; Eko, Eko, Aradia"* over and over. In one version, *Coven* members make efforts to disorient the Postulant by pushing them back and forth and sometimes turning them toward a new direction.

A bell is rung three times and the "Leader/Initiator" calls for the actions to cease—at which point the Postulant is turned toward the Leader (or *High Priestess*). The Leader (or *High Priestess*) kneels before the "Initiate" saying: *"In other religions, the postulant kneels, while the priest towers above him. But in the Arts Magical, we are taught to be humble, and we kneel to welcome them as we say..."*—and she continues speaking and administering the *"Rite of Fivefold Blessing/Kiss"* (feet, knees, and so on).

Next, the "measure" is taken—a facet seldom observed in modern traditions. It is theorized that a body measure recorded and maintained by the *Coven*—along with personal nail clipping and hair —could be used for future magical purposes to either help or harm a member. It is not generally considered wise to enforce continuing membership against their will; but what if the *Witch* were to betray her *Coven?* Today it is considered a "symbolic rite," although those experienced in practical magick will undoubtedly observe all the significance held between the lines.

So, the "Sponsor" hands the *High Priestess* an eight-foot length of string, who then announces that she "*will now take your measure.*" With the assistance of another *Priestess*, she takes a "measure" of the Initiate's height; stretching the string from the feet (where it is held by the assistant) to the head. The measured spot is pinched off and another assistant uses the *Boline* (or white-handled knife) to cut the string. Additional measures are taken with the string: around the head; around the chest; around the hips—and each time a knot is tied to mark it.[†] Finally, it is wound up and placed on the *Altar.*

The final portion[‡] of the original *Gardnerian* "First Degree Initiation," is a formal introduction to the "Elemental Tools." It is sometimes unclear whether or not an *Initiate* would have constructed all of their own tools at this juncture of development, or

---

[†] A note from personal experience: each of the three measures are made starting with the same end of the string. If you were to start from each new measure knot, it would typically require a greater length of string.

[‡] Editor's Note: It is an interesting point of fact that the present author has refrained from any instructions regarding "ritual scourging," which is actually quite paramount to *Gardner's Book of Shadows.*

if this is simply a demonstration by the *High Priestess* using *Coven* materials. We do, however, know that by the "Second Degree Initiation," a *Witch* must have found, made or been gifted with components for a complete set of personal tools—which are consecrated by the *High Priestess* and then returned to the *Initiate* for them to demonstrate their use at the Quarters during that *Rite of Initiation*.

The "Second Degree Initiation," in *Gardnerian Wicca*, is essentially identical to the steps of the first (and those illustrated within the "Outer Court" degrees of the *Elven Fellowship Circle of Magick*)—but this time, as stated above, the *Initiate* demonstrates use of their "Elemental Tools." In Gardner's version, it is also during the "Second Degree Initiation" that a *Witch* takes on, and is introduced to the *Coven* as, their "magical name." The *Initiate* is then taken to each Quarter and announced to the "*Lords of the Watchtowers*" by their new name as a "*Consecrated Witch*" and *Priestess* (or *Priest*).

The Oath taken for this *Rite* goes: "*Repeat thy new name after me, saying: 'I,* [name]*, swear upon my mother's womb, and by my honor among men and my Brothers and Sisters of the Art, that I will never reveal, to any at all, any of the secrets of the Art, except it be to a worthy person, properly prepared, in the center of a Magic Circle such as I* *am now in. This I swear by my hopes of salvation, my past lives, and my hopes of future ones to come; and I dedicate myself and my measure to utter destruction if I break my solemn Oath.*"

A final distinct point of Gardner's "Second Degree Initiation" is unique in contrast to the traditional "Italio-Celtic" flavor his *Book of Shadows* usually demonstrates: "*The Descent of the Goddess Inanna-Ishtar,*" which is dramatically reenacted—and quite blatantly Mesopotamian (Sumerian/Babylonian) in origin. This winks loudly to a little-known legend regarding true origins of the "Witch-Cult" among the "Priestesses of Inanna," even extending back to pre-Babylonian "Uruk Sumerians" (*c. 4th millennium BC*).∞

It is at this point that we see a distinction in the developing literature for *Witchcraft* through the 20th century, because in many instances, a reader may discover the "*Descent of the Goddess to the Underworld*" used in substitution for Gardner's own "Third Degree Initiation."[43] One reason this com-

---

∞ For additional details regarding Mesopotamia, refer to the Mardukite library titles dedicated to such topics, including: "*The Complete Anunnaki Bible*" and "*The Sumerian Legacy,*" both of which are contained in the Master Edition hardcover anthology: "*Necronomicon: The Complete Anunnaki Legacy*" by Joshua Free.

43 As seen, for example, in *Lady Sheba's Book of*

monly occurred is because *Initiates* often opted to prematurely break away from early *Covens* before being released with a "Third Degree Initiation" to officially go an start their own. Many other *Covens* and *Books of Shadows* released in the 20th Century have also been based, in part, by second-hand knowledge from diverse sources that were simply incorporated into contemporary presentations of *Wicca* and *Witchcraft* today.*

At the start of the "Third Degree Initiation," according to the original *Gardnerian Book of Shadows*, the High Priestess ties the "Magus" (High Priest) to the Altar for a scourging, then he is released and does the same to her. This is apparently quite common in the old "traditionalist" flavor of *Wicca*. The Quarters are addressed announcing the *Initiation* of the new *Priest* or *Priestess* and then the "Magus" says something to the effect of *"Assist me to erect the Ancient Altar,"* at which point the *Priestess* lies down in the center of the Magic Circle and arranges the appendages of their body in the styling of a pentagram.[44] After which, a

---

Shadows, published by Jessie Wicker Bell in 1972.

* This became increasingly common starting in the early 1970's with the work of Alex and Maxine Sanders—and increased dissemination of *"Alexandrian Wicca."*

44 The actual instructions read: "Priestess lies down in such a way that her vagina is approximately at

series of "kisses" and "blessings" are exchanged, saying *"Make open the path of intelligence between us. For these truly are the five points of fellowship..."* and so on—as with "The Great Rite."

---

the center of the Circle."—*Gardnerian Book of Shadows.*

NANCY'S BOOK OF SHADOWS

A Tribute to
"THE CRAFT"

NANCY'S BOOK OF SHADOWS
-or-
Everything I Need to Know About The Craft, I Learned From
"THE CRAFT"
(Merlyn Stone, Summer-Autumn '98)

It may seem strange how much time and attention has been taken on *Notebooks* for *The Witch's Handbook* this year,* and yet unlike the original treatment of *The Sorcerer's Handbook*, very little has been directed here toward the subject of "*magick*" directly. This is not an oversight. For one, it is basically assumed that those receiving this material will have immediate access to *The Sorcerer's Handbook* first edition. Secondly, it is already expected that material from the former will be combined with this one to compose a more access-

---

*   Each main section of *The Witch's Handbook* was originally prepared as a separate installment (during the course of a year) for inclusion into the greater body of work known as "*1998 Book of Shadows*" for *Elven Fellowship Circle of Magick*.

ible third edition of the *Handbook*.[‡]

More importantly, when one considers the subject of true *Witchcraft*—especially as it is demonstrated in the 20th century—we are really concerned with a "pagan" (or "neopagan") "*religious tradition*" far more than we are dealing with a particular brand, flavor or style of "magick." As we have seen from various installments distributed for our "*1998 Book of Shadows*" this year, the development of "modern" *Witchcraft* is really a combination of reviving customs and traditions from the "Ancient Ways" (or what many now consider "*Ye Olde Tyme Religion*") coupled with several centuries of ongoing reinvestigation into archaic "occult philosophies" and the *Arts of Magic*. In today's society, the proliferation and propagation of these efforts takes on many forms...

◊ ◊ ◊ ◊ ◊ ◊

There are some in the pagan community that remain upset over the 1996 Columbia Pictures release of "*The Craft*." It does, however, arrive in the mainstream during a critical turning point in

---

‡   Facets of the first edition "*Sorcerer's Handbook*" (Spring 1998) and the second edition (as the "*Witch's Handbook*" or "*1998 Book of Shadows*") were combined for the *Sorcerer's Notebook*, released publicly in Autumn 1998 as the third edition of *Sorcerer's Handbook*, which was distributed globally as such through all of 1999.

the widespread development of "New Age" practices and the modern *Witchcraft* movement in general. Although the movie does illustrate several rites inspired by Ceremonial Magic (including some facets described as such within our "*1998 Book of Shadows*"), semantically speaking, very little actual "*Wiccan*" tradition is expressed—perhaps, most notably, the blatant absence of emphasis on a "goddess"-centric magical system or ever popular "*grrrrl power*"-type we might otherwise expect.[45]

The movie follows events taking place after "Sarah" (*played by Robin Tunney, later to star in "End of Days"*) moves to Los Angeles with her parents and transfers to a new Catholic School. There, she finds herself initiated into a small *coven* led by "Nancy Downs" (*the amazing Fairuza Balk, who starred in "Worst Witch" and "Return to Oz" as a child*), with two friends "Rochelle" (*Rachel True*) and "Bonnie" (*Neve Campbell, known from "Scream" and "Wild Things"*). Needless to say for those who have already seen the film: things take a bit of a turn when Sarah's incorporation apparently advances or increases power of the group beyond the temperance and wisdom of its members to properly use it.

---

45 Portions of this paragraph are rewritten as the entree for "*The Craft*" found in "*The Great Magickal Arcanum*" by Joshua Free.

The Craft debuted in theaters just after Beltane 1996 based on a script treatment developed by *Peter Filardi* (best known for writing "*Flatliners*") —although the final screenplay was amended by joint-writer and film-director *Andrew Fleming*, with some assistance by a technical consultant, *Pat Devin*, a member of a *Wiccan* organization known as "*Covenant of the Goddess*" (*CoG*).

Pat Devin is not only a "*Dianic Wiccan*" herself, she serves for the public-relations office at *CoG*. She was interviewed by Llewellyns New Worlds magazine-catalog regarding her participation on the set of *The Craft* shortly after its release. It was also noted in interviews and production commentary notes that *Robin Tunney* had at least some independent interest and knowledge in the subject of *Wicca* prior to the movie and *Fairuza Balk* was certainly no stranger to the *Craft*, having a family background in many of its facets and going on to purchase *Panpipes Magickal Marketplace*—the oldest occult shop in Los Angeles, established in 1971—mainly to save it from going out of business at the time.

There are, of course, many "Hollywood-ized" elements found in *The Craft*, which are unique to its own take on magic and are included purely to "put on a good show." That being said, there is a considerable amount of effective data that may be drawn from the film and of which has served, in some ways, as an elementary introduction for young girls and boys of this generation that are interested in "*magic*" and "*witchcraft*" and see this work as a type of "Rite of Passage" in itself—a means for an individual to come into their own power. Those traditions that deal heavily in "Self-empowerment" are predicted to be on the "rise" well into the 21st Century as more of the "up and coming" population begins to direct its attentions away from the religious institutions that have set up authoritarian intermediaries to the truth.

◊ ◊ ◊ ◊ ◊ ◊ ◊

NANCY'S BOOK OF SHADOWS: AN APPENDIX

(Practical Notes from "THE CRAFT")

[0:45]* <u>OPENING CHANT</u>

> *Now is the time; this is the hour.*
> *Ours is the magic; ours is the power.*

Chanted by each individual of the coven simultaneously to attune the members. [The girls are seen seated around a small circular table/Altar on an outdoor patio space that is decorated with magical tools, stones and many candles.]

---

* Approximate time-stamp from the film, starting with Universal logo.

[*6:30*]   A FOUR-MEMBER ELEMENTAL COVEN-STRUCTURE

A new wholeness and with it a new balance;
Earth, Air, Fire and Water.

The "Quarters"† or directions are treated by their "Elemental" properties in ritual magic. A "Circle" is correlated to symbolism of four "Elemental directions"—and each station may be effectively represented by a member of the coven. Although magic can be practiced by any number of individuals, there is a certain symmetrical balance in a four-member coven-structure. [Bonnie is reading to the other girls from *The Witches' Almanac* and predicting they might finally meet a "fourth" member.]

[*14:45*]   PERSONAL BOOK OF SHADOWS

You put spells and power thoughts in it.

A personal notebook or "Book of Shadows" is kept to record one's own magical journey (like a diary) and also to include any rites one has written —and to copy the group rituals and liturgy practiced within one's coven. [Bonnie attempts to convince Sarah to steal a blank "Book of Shadows" from an occult shop.]

---

† · Referred to as *corners* in the film.

[*18:15*] PATRON DEITIES FOR THE COVEN TRADITION

Maybe he'll really listen now...

Witchcraft, as a religion, holds a certain concept of "Divinity," however unique or individual that may be. [The group gathers in a park to educate Sarah about "*Manon*"—a specific persona of Divinity that the coven is dedicated to. The name chosen for the movie was intentionally fictitious.]

[*29:15*] ELEMENTAL CHANT

Earth. Air. Fire. Water.

Chanted by each of the four members of the coven, while seated in a circle, holding hands. All four simultaneously chant "*Earth. Air. Fire. Water.*" in total four times, then each speaks only their own respective element four times (or eight times). [The four girls take their first major outing together, traveling by bus to a rural grove set in a meadow.]

[*29:30*] RITE OF THE BLADE

—*It is better that you should rush upon this blade than enter the circle with fear in your heart. How do you enter?*
—*With perfect love and perfect trust.*

Similar to the original *Gardnerian Initiations:** be

———

* Refer to "*Rites of Initiation*" (*Spring 1998*)

fore entering the working area, each member of the coven stands in line waiting to be admitted into the Circle. The dagger/*Athame* is held up to their chest, the challenge is said, passwords are given, and finally the passing a kiss (the third password). [On film, Rochelle initiates Bonnie; Bonnie initiates Nancy; and Nancy initiates Sarah. Nancy then takes the dagger/*Athame* and raises it up, pointed to the sky, speaks "*As above,*" and then plunges it into the ground with everyone saying "*So below.*"]

[*30:30*] <u>COMMUNION OF WINE</u>

> *I drink of my sisters*
> *and I take into myself (stated intention).*

Group magic or Circle magic may be a combination of coven energy, collected from all members and then channeled toward individual intentions. [Wine is poured into a communal *Chalice*. Each of the girls pricks their finger with a pin (or needle) and pinches a drop of blood into the Wine.[†] Rochelle begins the rotation, stating: "*I drink of my sisters and ask for the ability to not hate those who hate me...*" and then she takes a drink. The *Chalice* is passed to each in turn to do similar. Nancy completes the cycle and says, "*Blessed Be,*" which is then echoed by the others.]

----

section of the *BoS*.

[†] Included in this review, but not necessarily recommended for practice.

THE LOVE SPELL

This spell is to be practiced for seven days in succession, preferably during the waxing cycle of the Moon and beginning on a Friday. Each day, the two candles are moved closer to each other.

The Circle is cast and the witch petitions their patron deity and says, "*Hear my plea to you; my plea of love for ___ and their desire.*" A talisman may be employed here, and the words spoken: "*Sator, Arepo, Tenet, Opera, Rotas. Iah. Iah. Iah. I summon to me what all I desire.*" Light the candle representing you (on the right-side or projective side of the *Altar*) and say: "*This flame burns as does my spirit. The love I have for ___ is great and burns deep within my being.*" Light the candle representing the target of the spell (on the left-side or receptive side of the *Altar*), saying: "*This is the heart and soul of ___, whom I see and conjure a picture of before me.*" In your Mind's Eye, see an image of the other person smiling and coming toward you with an open embrace. Push that image into your body and say, "*The love ___ has for me grows as does this flame. It burns as does this candle and is forever drawn to me. Great is the love I have for ___ and great is the love ___ has for me.*" Light a third (red) candle and say: "*I draw ___ to me; the one toward the other; and the thought of me shall be constant.*"

Release the energy and direct it toward the target, saying: "*My spell is upon you ___, and my desire for you is great. May love blossom and sweeten between us. My spell is upon you ___, I have directed the powers of the Universe to coax you into my arms.*" [Sarah uses magic to cause her high school crush, Chris (*played by Skeet Ulrich*), to fall helplessly "in love" with her.]

[*48:30*] THROWING A GLAMOUR

> *Glamour—to throw an illusion so real*
> *as to fool an onlooker*
> *is one of the oldest forms of magic.*

As its name implies, a "glamour" is an illusion—but this is not unique, because the "persona" or "façade" you display outward in the Physical Universe is already an illusion of sorts. Furthermore, what you project as Self on a physical level also has its influence from the emotional, psychological and spiritual systems of beingness.

This spell should be practiced at night, or at dusk or twilight, preferably on a Friday or Saturday (evoking influences of Venus and Saturn) during the waxing phase or on a Full Moon. Some versions specify the New Moon.

You will require a red candle (charisma) and a green candle (Venus and beauty), a mirror (preferably black, or some other skrying speculum, like a crystal ball) and a stone amulet to "charge" and "program" the changes, which is worn afterward.

Set yourself comfortably in front of the mirror with the candles on either side of you, consecrated and lit. This is the only source of illumination that should affect the Magic Circle, but the actual flames should not be reflectively visible in the mirror. Gaze into this speculum and allow the Mind to clear, then Will and see the desired changes. Magically burn, impress or charge this image into the amulet with a verbal affirmation, such as: "*What I will is the face I wear.*"[46]

[On film, Sarah is seated before a piece of white paper marked with a pentagram in black marker. It is sprinkled with herbs and pink flowers and encircled with feathers. A single pink candle is lit in the center of the star. She places her open palm hand face down above the candle and says: "*This is to feel.*" She moves her hand to the left side of the candle, saying: "*This is to be*"—and then covers her face with both hands, "*Shape and form it for all to see. By the power of three time three, as*

---

46 In "*Great Magickal Arcanum,*" this is followed
    by conjuring the spiritual hierarchy commanded
    by the entity "*Magoth,*" of which a roll-call of
    names—*Nacheron, Natolico, Mesaf, Masadul,
    Sappipas, Faturab, Ubarim, Rotor* and *Arabim*—
    are also summoned. The amulet is then held in
    the left hand and run down the face, top to
    bottom.

I will it, so shall it be."]⁴⁷

[*52:30*] <u>THE LAW OF THREEFOLD RETURN</u>

> *Life keeps a balance on its own.*
> *Whatever you send out*
> *you get back times three.*

Wicca acknowledges energetic repercussions of personal actions in a way similar to the "*karma*" of Eastern traditions, evolving to a popularized statement about "threefold returns." Prior to this, Gardnerian Wicca emphasized "As you harm none, do what thou will," amending Crowley's own sentiment of simply "Do what thou will." [Occult shop owner, Lirio (*played by Assumpta Serna*), attempts to educate the girls on the ethics of magic and energy handling. Meanwhile, Nancy is enamored by an animate illustrations in a book, titled "*Invocation of the* Spirit"—which is really a copy of A.E. Waite's "*Book of (Black) Ceremonial Magic*."]

[*53:30*] <u>MAY'S EVE (BELTANE) RITE</u>
    <u>—"INVOKING THE SPIRIT"</u>

EXT. BEACH - NIGHT
Bonnie finishes laying a ring of stones in the

---

47 Author's Note: I found a modern "three-times-three banishing" spell buried in the back of Timothy Roderick's "*Dark Moon Mysteries*," but it applies to a later scene far better than this one.

> *sand.*
> *Nancy starts a fire in the middle.*
> *Sarah finishes lighting a circle of black*
> *   candles.*
> *She looks at the snake in the jar...* *

The ritual practiced on the beach contains many elements of ceremonial magic (that are referenced within *The Witch's Handbook* sections), particularly the "elemental" attributes and "calls" to the "Corners" (Watchtowers). [Rochelle carries a "goldfish" in a bag; Bonnie carries a "butterfly" in a jar; Sarah carries a "bird" in a small cage; Nancy carries a larger jar containing a "snake."]

On screen, the ritual script begins with Nancy: "*Hail to the Guardians of the Watchtower of the East; The powers of Air and Invention; Hear (us).*" Then, Bonnie: "*Hail to the Guardians of the Watchtower of the South; The powers of Fire and Feeling; Hear (us).*" Rochelle: "*Hail to the Guardians of the Watchtower of the West; The Powers of Water and Intuition; Hear (us).*" Finally, Sarah: "*Hail to the Guardians of the Watchtower of the North; By the powers of Mother and Earth; Hear (us).*"

---

* Excerpting a draft of the screenplay. The scene was shot in Malibu, at Leo Carrillo Beach. According to rumors, when Fairuza Balk (Nancy) began speaking the incantations, the film crew lost power (from their generators).

Nancy continues the incantation: "*Aid us in our magical working on this May's Eve. Serpent of old, ruler of the deep, guardian of the bitter sea— show us your glory, show us your power. We pray of thee. We invoke thee. O serpent one, hear our calls; hear our prayers. Ancient wise one, teach us thy ways. We summon and stir thee. Lend us your powers. Show us your glory. We invoke thee! We invoke thee!*"

[72:15] BINDING SPELL

> *I bind you, ___, from doing harm;*
> *Harm against other people*
> *And harm against yourself.*

A lot of nonsense is written about "white witchcraft" versus "black magic" and so forth. Magic is magic. But, needless to say, there are *Witches* that would use these abilities to cause harm. Binding spells are treated as ethical means for defending against "malevolent magic" or "baneful intentions" These rites sidestep negative kickback because it simply "returns" or "deflects" the originally directed energy back to its sender, adding to it no ill-Will. [Sarah cuts an image of Nancy out of a group photo and proceeds to wrap a white ribbon around it as she makes her incantation.]

[86:30] THREE-TIMES-THREE

> *By the powers of three times three;*
> *Make them see, make them see.*

Using the dagger/*Athame*, inscribe an appropriate representative word or name near the bottom of a black candle. Charge it with residual negative energies that have been attached to you from the target. Tie a length of white cotton twine securely at the bottom and then proceed to wrap it around the candle, moving upwards counter-clockwise, while visualizing a deflective mirrored sphere encircling your body.

The incantation suggested by Timothy Roderick in "*Dark Moon Mysteries*" (published the same year "*The Craft*" was released) is: "*Three times three, as ye have sown; Is thine to reap, thy harvest grown. For best, for worst, for praise or chide; The Gods alone your fate decide.*" Continue wrapping the candle until the twine reaches the top, then saturate it with lamp oil. Place it in a cauldron that has its bottom lined with sand (to hold the candle in place and also for fire protection) and burn the candle until it has completely melted away. Bury any of the remainder.

[Sarah defends herself against further attacks by Rochelle and Bonnie by projecting a glamour to show them the threefold repercussions of their actions. She combines this with a binding incantation to battle Nancy later.]

FINIS

The Perfect Companion to
The Witch's Handbook

THE SORCERER'S HANDBOOK
A Complete Guide to Practical Magick
21st Anniversary Collector's Edition
by Joshua Free writing as Merlyn Stone

Available in Hardcover for the First Time!

THE ORIGINAL HARDCOVER 2-VOLUME SET

SUMERIAN RELIGION

Introducing the Anunnaki Gods
of Mesopotamian Neopaganism

Mardukite Liber-50

by Joshua Free

BABYLONIAN MYTH & MAGIC

Spiritual Traditions and Mysticism
in Mesopotamian Anunnaki Religion

Mardukite Liber-51+E

by Joshua Free

SYSTEMOLOGY BASICS HARDCOVER SET

THE POWER OF ZU

Applying Mardukite Zuism and
Systemology to Everyday Life
Systemology Liber-S1-Z
based on a lecture series
by Joshua Free

THE WAY INTO THE FUTURE

A Handbook for the New Human
Systemology Liber-S1-W
collected works mini-anthology
by Joshua Free

SYSTEMOLOGY
The Pathway to Self-Honesty

GO FURTHER AND BE

CRYSTAL CLEAR

CRYSTAL CLEAR

(Handbook for Seekers)

Mardukite Systemology Liber-2B
by Joshua Free

Take control of your destiny
and chart the first steps
toward your own spiritual evolution.
Realize new potentials of the
Human Condition with
a Self-guiding handbook for
Self-Processing toward
Self-Actualization
in Self-Honesty using actual
techniques and training
provided for the coveted
"Mardukite Systemology Grade-III
Self-Defragmentation Course Program"
—once only available
directly and privately from
the underground Systemology Society.

Discover the amazing power behind the
applied spiritual technology
used for counseling and advisement in
the tradition of Mardukite Zuism.

SILVER ANNIVERSARY

19 95   20 20

JOSHUA FREE

PUBLISHED BY THE **JOSHUA FREE** IMPRINT REPRESENTING

The Founding Church of Mardukite Zuism

THE JOSHUA FREE IMPRINT
JFI PUBLICATIONS

MARDUKITE
ZUISM

mardukite.com

www.ingramcontent.com/pod-product-compliance
Lightning Source LLC
Chambersburg PA
CBHW011236120626
46549CB00009B/3287